Adversity, Adoption and
Afterwards
A mid-life follow-up study of
women adopted from Hong Kong

Adversity, Adoption and Afterwards
A mid-life follow-up study of women adopted from Hong Kong

Julia Feast, Margaret Grant,
Alan Rushton and
John Simmonds with
Carolyn Sampeys

Published by British Association
for Adoption & Fostering
(BAAF)
Saffron House
6–10 Kirby Street
London EC1N 8TS
www.baaf.org.uk

Charity registration 275689 (England and Wales)
and SC039337 (Scotland)

British Library Cataloguing in Publication Data
A catalogue record for this book is available
from the British Library

ISBN 978 1 907585 64 7

Project management by Shaila Shah,
Director of Publications, BAAF
Photograph on cover posed by models
Designed by Helen Joubert Designs
Typeset by Avon DataSet Ltd, Bidford on Avon
Printed in Great Britain by TJ International
Trade distribution by Turnaround Publisher Services,
Unit 3, Olympia Trading Estate, Coburg Road,
London N22 6TZ

BAAF is the leading UK-wide membership
organisation for all those concerned with
adoption, fostering and child care issues.

Contents

Contents

List of tables

List of figures

Acknowledgements

First and foremost, we would like to thank the women who participated in this study. They generously gave their time and shared their thoughts and feelings about their experiences throughout their lives. Without them, this project would not have been possible and we are indebted to them. We are delighted that the project coincided with the development of the UK Hong Kong Adult Adoptees Network and that the study played a role by putting the women in touch with one another when this was requested.

We would also like to thank our pilot group: Trina Banks, Annette Harvey, Alex Kenny, Susie Maslin and Karen Moir, who patiently worked with us to refine the research materials used in the study.

Our enormous thanks go to The Nuffield Foundation which funded the project and particularly to Sharon Witherspoon MBE who has been a great support throughout.

We were fortunate to have a group of highly experienced research interviewers who carried out this complex task with sensitivity and expertise: Jenny Castle, Erica Peltier, Jenny Setterington, Janet Smith, Rose Wallace and Elizabeth Webb.

We are grateful to Maria Affinito, Professor Toni Bifulco, Margaret Bryer, Jenny Castle, Dr Helen Fisher, Dr Annie Lau, Professor Barbara Maughan, Kate Roach, Professor Penny Roy and Professor Peter Selman, all members of our Research Advisory Group, ably chaired by Caroline Thomas. They offered consistent expert interest and support throughout the study and all of them contributed in different ways above and beyond what is normally expected of an advisory group. Dr Morven Leese deserves special thanks for her expertise and advice on the statistical analysis. We are also grateful to Clare Flach for her help in the early stages of the project. We would like to thank Dr Elizabeth Monck for her close scrutiny and detailed feedback on draft chapters.

Several current and former members of BAAF staff also deserve thanks, not least our administrators Mary Bollan, Genevieve Cameron, Caitlin O'Neill Gutierrez and Danielle Sawyer. Catherine Walker meticulously researched the background to the Hong Kong Adoption Project and contributed much of the material that forms the basis of Chapter 1. Dan Marsh and Gareth Allen helped us with IT support and Ola Sokoya with advice on the challenging budgetary issues. We would also like to acknowledge Lucy Abercrombie, Sheila Hayler, Simonetta Mullany, Amanda Priest and Karen Wilkins who transcribed the interviews from the study.

One of the unique aspects of this study is that it has benefited enormously from the hard work and commitment of a number of people who have contributed their time as volunteers in a range of roles: Laura Batatota, Dan Brooks, Alexandra Conroy Harris, Ellie Dalton-Loveland, Rebecca Dean, Qing Gu, Holly Holder, Susana Ihenacho, Irena Lyczkowska, Steven McMillin, Rachel Neal, Pesh Patel, Sarah Patel, David Setterington, Luke Tripp and Catherine Webb. Dr Gill Clark deserves a special mention for her commitment over the many months it took to locate the participants. Her knowledge of archives and public records was invaluable and contributed greatly to our success in tracing the women.

Last but by no means least, Shaila Shah from BAAF's Publications team has turned our draft chapters into models of clarity, consistency and sense with undeserved (on our part) goodwill, expertise and speed.

The Nuffield Foundation

The Nuffield Foundation is an endowed charitable trust that aims to improve social well-being in the widest sense. It funds research and innovation in education and social policy and also works to build capacity in education, science and social science research. The Nuffield Foundation has funded this project, but the views expressed are those of the authors and not necessarily those of the Foundation. More information is available at www.nuffieldfoundation.org.

Note

Comparison group general population data were obtained from the 1958 National Child Development Study (NCDS) 1999/2000 and 2004 sweeps. This UK Data Archive is administered by the Economic and Social Data Service (ESDS) at the University of Essex.

Notes about the authors

Julia Feast OBE
Policy, Research & Development Consultant, BAAF

Julia Feast is the Policy, Research and Development Consultant for BAAF. She is an experienced social worker and researcher. Before starting at BAAF, she managed the Children's Society's Post-Adoption and Care Counselling Research Project. In the past she has worked as a local authority social worker and team manager, and also as a Children's Guardian and Reporting Officer.

Julia has a particular interest in the identity and information rights and needs of adopted people, post-care adults and donor-conceived people. Apart from the British Chinese Adoption Study, she has been involved in two other major research studies on the subject of adoption, search and reunion, and also one on access to care records for post-care adults. Her publications include: *Adoption, Search and Reunion: The long-term experience of adopted adults*, *The Adoption Triangle Revisited: A study of adoption, search and reunion experiences*, *The Adoption Reunion Handbook* and *A Childhood on Paper: Accessing the child care files of former looked after children in the UK*.

Margaret Grant
Senior Researcher, BAAF

Margaret Grant is a Senior Researcher at BAAF. She has worked on the British Chinese Adoption Study since 2007 and has been involved in all aspects of the study. She has previously worked on projects including testing reading skill interventions for children in foster care; the use of video in profiling children for family finding; and the experiences of unaccompanied asylum-seeking children and their foster carers.

Alan Rushton

Visiting Professor, Institute of Psychiatry, King's College London

Alan Rushton spent many years as a social worker in both child and adult mental health services in the UK and Canada. For over 25 years, he was Director of the MSc programme in Mental Health Social Work at the Institute of Psychiatry, King's College London, where he continues as Visiting Professor. He has been engaged in follow-up studies of older, abused children adopted from care and in predictors of placement outcome.

He has published many academic papers and several books via BAAF, including *Adoption Support Services for Families in Difficulty*, *Enhancing Adoptive Parenting: A test of effectiveness* and *Enhancing Adoptive Parenting: A parenting programme for use with adopters of challenging children*. He is currently a Trustee at the Post-Adoption Centre in London.

Dr John Simmonds

Director of Policy, Research & Development, BAAF

John Simmonds is Director of Policy, Research and Development at BAAF. Before starting at BAAF, he was head of the social work programmes at Goldsmiths College, University of London. He is a qualified social worker and has substantial experience in child protection, family placement and residential care settings. He has published widely, including co-editing with Gillian Schofield *The Child Placement Handbook*, and authoring *The Role of Special Guardianship: Best practice in permanency planning for children*, both published by BAAF. He recently completed a research project on unaccompanied asylum-seeking children in foster care with the University of York and is starting a new DfE-funded project on special guardianship, also with the University of York. He is the adoptive father of two children, now adults.

Dr Carolyn Sampeys

Dr Carolyn Sampeys, BM DRCOG MRCPCH, is a Community Paediatrician and Named Doctor for Adoption, Fostering and Looked After Children for Cardiff and Vale University Health Board. She acts as Medical Adviser in Adoption to Cardiff and the Vale of Glamorgan local authorities. Dr Sampeys is Chair of the BAAF UK Health Group Advisory Committee and past Chair of the BAAF Welsh Medical Group. She is also a BAAF Trustee. Carolyn has been instrumental in the development of multi-disciplinary "Children First" Teams for Looked After children in Cardiff and the Vale of Glamorgan and chairs the all-Wales Looked after Children's Health Exchange. She took the lead in writing Chapter 7.

Foreword

Professor Sir Michael Rutter

Research councils are notoriously reluctant to support studies into unusual groups or unusual circumstances on the grounds that they cannot be relevant for contemporary society. Fortunately, that is not the approach of the Nuffield Foundation, who realise that what is very different may provide a splendid "natural experiment" that allows variables that ordinarily go together to be teased apart. The British Chinese Adoption Study (BCAS) constituted just such an opportunity to understand better the consequences of intercountry adoption.

The book admirably sets the scene in terms of the situation in China/Hong Kong half a century ago together with the then prevailing views about adoption and child rearing. The book is well worth reading as a most interesting and informative piece of social history. There is also a succinct summary of what is known from other research into intercountry adoption (ICA) and the institutional experiences that gave rise to ICA. However, the main purpose of the book was to describe one particular study – the BCAS, and the remainder of my remarks will focus on that study.

In many respects, the most important point to make is that the BCAS provides an outstandingly impressive example of the huge advantages that derive from the combination of quantitative and qualitative research methods. The former has the strength of providing numerical findings on the extent to which groups differ on standardised scores or ratings of a range of variables but, particularly in unusual circumstances, it loses out on the personal meaning or individual feelings about personal experiences. That is just what qualitative interviewing provides. But what is really distinctive about the BCAS is the thoughtful integration of the two approaches. That has worked spectacularly well in a range of ways that are well described in the book.

The book is also well worth reading for the easy-to-read account of the planning that went into the study – dealing with matters involving samples, measures, participation and ethical issues. Most research reports provide a rather dry recital of these methodological issues but this book goes well beyond that in describing the thinking that went into the planning. The result was an astonishing success in tracing women with whom there had been no contact for many decades, and usually in gaining their full participation and co-operation. The book also brings out well the particular strengths of the recent sources available.

What about the findings? Bearing in mind the British Film Institute warning that the programme notes for their films give away some of the plot, I will seek simply to whet your appetite for reading the book by mentioning just a few of the gems in the findings. First, the adult outcomes of the adopted women were overall very positive. Their mental health, marriages, parenting and friendships all compared well with the British population and their educational attainments were markedly superior. Thus, about a third obtained a university degree. Second, even among those now currently doing well, there had been ups and downs over the years. This was not just a matter of opportunity but also the ways in which the women made use of what was available.

Third, there was substantial heterogeneity in outcomes – as found in all other studies. One feature that seemed relevant in that connection was the women's recollection of the parenting provided in the adoptive families. That is rather different from what has been found in other studies and there are inevitable uncertainties on the possibility of biases inherent in having to recall what happened many years ago. Nevertheless, the findings do highlight both the views on child rearing half a century ago that differ substantially from those prevailing today as well as the much weaker scrutiny of people applying to adopt in that era.

Fourth, both ethnic identification and exposure to racist attitudes and behaviour are discussed in a thoughtful way guided by both the empirical quantitative findings and the views expressed in the qualitative interviews. Finally, there is a helpful discussion of the policy and practice implications of the BCAS findings.

So, now, read on. The authors have provided a wonderfully riveting account of a highly unusual study from which all of us can learn a lot.

Preface

Early in 2004, the British Association for Adoption and Fostering (BAAF) was given access to the records of 106 Chinese children, now adults, who were placed for adoption with mainly English couples, in the UK, during the 1960s. These children had spent their early years in orphanages in Hong Kong and all but one were girls. The arrangements for the placement of these children had been made by International Social Service (ISS) through its branches in Hong Kong and the UK. The adoptive families had been selected and assessed by the National Children's Homes (NCH)[1] or Barnardo's, and these agencies supervised the adoption placements. The ISS UK adoption records relating to these children are intact and include standardised and non-standardised descriptions, in the words of the Hong Kong childcare workers and local medical staff, of the child's physical health and development. They also contain other observations of the time the children were cared for in the institutions including information about their transfer to and settling-in period with their adoptive families.

ISS UK granted BAAF permission to test the integrity of these data and to consider whether it would be feasible to undertake a study to retrospectively explore the long-term outcomes for this group of adopted children, now adults in middle age. An initial look at the files revealed that they provided an intriguing and valuable child welfare record. They were fairly well-ordered and consistent and contained a range of documents, such as typed and hand-written letters, official adoption forms, health and social records, photographs and even some newspaper articles. Some files were particularly bulky and contained lengthy correspondence between prospective adopters and ISS staff both before and after the placements.

We were aware that a selective study (51 adoptive parents and 53

---

1 Now called Action for Children

children from the same cohort i.e. about half the total sample studied in this report) had been undertaken by Bagley and Young in 1979 with a follow-up study in 1988. There have been no further studies of the outcomes for these children in adulthood particularly in important areas such as education, employment, adult relationships, parenting and mental and physical health. The potential benefits of undertaking a further follow-up study, to explore the lifelong implications of their adoption and the outcomes for this group, were very apparent and identifying a comparison group a particularly important aspect of this.

In 2007, BAAF undertook a feasibility study to interrogate the data held on the ISS UK files, an exercise made possible by funding from the Nuffield Foundation. It became clear that there was significant scope for a quantitative and qualitative follow-up study with a comparison group from the 1958 National Child Development Study, as outlined in Chapter 3. Further funding was secured from the Nuffield Foundation for this purpose. Files relating to the adoption of 106 children were available from ISS. A total of 100 women were selected for the follow-up study, with six excluded because the placement did not match the study's criteria, for example, because it was a private fostering arrangement or a step-parent adoption. Fifteen of the adoptive families had adopted two unrelated girls each through the ISS programme.

The study seeks to explore a range of questions. For example, what happened to the girls after they left the orphanage? Was the adoption successful in promoting their development when they had had such an atypical start in life? If so, what protective factors were associated with successful outcomes? What happened to them when they became young adults? What is life like for them now? What was the range of their experiences – were they much the same as other women or were there vast differences? Another core strand of the study is the examination of how the participants viewed and experienced their Chinese heritage and appearance, given that they have spent four or five decades of life (mostly) in the UK. How do they identify themselves? Does their sense of belonging to their communities relate to their psychological health? How do they think others see them? What difficulties have they encountered and what do they see as the benefits of their heritage?

The study has used reliable, previously tested questionnaires to measure various aspects of well-being, mental health and self-worth. The use of standardised measures has also enabled important comparisons to be made with other studies, which aid our understanding of how these women's experiences may be similar to and different from these of other adopted and non-adopted women raised in the UK. The study also offers the rare opportunity of pulling together and analysing information from the early orphanage years, the women's subsequent lives in the UK, and their current psychological and social status. The extent to which early adversity, especially lack of personalised care, creates problematic developmental pathways has been a longstanding question for those interested in human development.

The study has generated a large amount of data of interest to a wide range of audiences, both academic and professional, and also to those interested in and affected by adoption. This book presents the main findings of the study; additionally, a number of papers and presentations are being prepared to report on further aspects of the research. It combines the initial analysis of some of the key outcome findings with a qualitative analysis of the face-to-face interviews with the women, interviews that were particularly rich in detail and which provide evocative and compelling stories of the course of these women's lives.

Adoption is inevitably associated with major transformations – the circumstances in which the child was "given up" and placed away from birth family members and then for adoption, the characteristics of adoptive family life, the similarities and differences between adopted children, and the significance of the status of an adoptive identity and the losses and gains this brings. The implications are even greater for those children who cross national borders (geographically, culturally and linguistically) to be adopted. It is this that gives this study a strong human interest element, extending its appeal beyond a specific interest in adoption.

The generosity of this group of women in sharing their experiences with us has been enormous. As well as giving up their time, they have trusted us with personal information about their lives and their views. For some this has involved recounting painful memories and describing experiences that were complex and multi-dimensional. This is balanced against others' memories of happy childhoods and fulfilling lives. For some, taking part in the study – and indeed finding out that there were other girls placed for adoption from similar origins and in the same way – has had a surprising impact on their lives. We are delighted that the study has coincided with the development of a global network of women adopted from Hong Kong, so that those who choose to can make connections with others who share similar early experiences.

What is reported here reinforces the view that adversity, resilience, opportunity and constraint walk hand in hand for most human beings. Reliable findings can be reported about the factors found to be significant over the life course of the women and this study will make an important contribution to our understanding of these factors. In addition, there are individual stories, each one of which is remarkable for what it conveys of the richness of human experience.

1 Historical overview of the British Chinese Adoption Study

Adoption is a powerful subject that can touch the hearts and minds of a wide range of people in society and not just those who have a direct personal connection with it. It can evoke a range of feelings and strong personal views because of the losses and gains and the joys and tribulations that can be involved.

Adoption in the UK has taken many twists and turns during its history. When adoption was first legalised in England and Wales (1926), Scotland (1930) and Northern Ireland (1929), it was intended to address the serious problems that had arisen about the large number of young children who could not be cared for by their parents because of the First World War, a major flu epidemic from 1918–1920, and the unacceptability of illegitimacy in society. The first Adoption and Children Act enacted in 1926 was designed to regulate the placement of children and particularly to give them legitimate and lasting status in their adoptive family (Simmonds, 2012).

However, legislation alone could not dispel the many ethical and moral dilemmas that have been raised about adoption over the years. For example, there have been real concerns about the extent to which adoptions up to the 1970s resulted from the pressure placed on unmarried mothers to relinquish their children as a consequence of society's attitude towards single parenthood at that time. In subsequent decades, strenuous and controversial debates have taken place about the legality and ethics of the adoption of children from the care system without the consent of their birth families (contested adoptions) (Ryburn, 1992; Mason and Selman, 1997; Murch *et al*, 1993). In the 1960s, there were debates about whether black children could be adopted by white couples, and later, whether it was even right to place black and mixed heritage children in transracial placements (Kirton, 2000). The early 1970s also saw the questioning of the belief that a "new start" or "clean break" following an adoption was the best approach. Instead, it was argued, that adopted people should be given the right to gain access to their records and to information about their origins (Howe and Feast, 2000; Keating, 2009).

At the centre of all these debates are the thousands of children who have grown up in families other than those into which they were born. In the case of intercountry adoption, the life-changing implications may be heightened, as children grow up not just in a different family but also in a different country and culture with all the challenges that brings. This study examines the lives of one such group of children, now women in their 40s and 50s, who were born in Hong Kong and went on to be adopted by families in the UK.

The socio-economic context leading to the Hong Kong adoptions

In October 1949, the Chinese Communist party established the People's Republic of China following four years of civil war that had resulted in a steady flow of migration from the Chinese mainland to Hong Kong. In the years following the declaration of the Communist republic, amidst ongoing political and economic instability, thousands of Chinese civilians chose to "vote with their feet" and immigration into Hong Kong remained high as the colony seemed to offer economic opportunities that the mainland did not. From a modest population of 5,000 in 1841 at the start of British rule, by 1961 the population had risen sharply to about three million (Hong Kong Council of Social Service, 1961).

It is estimated that by 1956, 700,000 people from mainland China had become refugees in Hong Kong, with a further 10,000 to 15,000 arriving each month (Hong Kong Government Annual Report, 1956 cited by International Social Service New York, 1958). By 1961, the Hong Kong Council of Social Service reported that nearly half the three-million-strong population could be refugees – 'a proportion of the uprooted exceeded by no other country in the world' with five births for every death in the city (Hong Kong Council of Social Service, 1961). An inordinately high birth rate of up to 2,000 children being born per week in 1961 was accompanied by a high incidence of child abandonment. A report from ISS in New York in 1958 suggested that:

There are an unlimited number of children urgently needing help and assistance of all kinds . . . There is no accurate estimate of the number of orphans available for adoption. Their number increases day by day. (ISS NY, 1958)

In 1959, 1960 and 1961, the number of children found "abandoned" was 229, 145, and 128 respectively (Hong Kong Council of Social Services, 1961). The Hong Kong Council of Social Service (1961) described the rocketing population numbers as 'an economic miracle of survival'. Yet this "economic miracle" was not initially matched by an accompanying social welfare provision for the growing population; hospital space and trained medical staff were in short supply and were insufficient to provide for the children's health needs. Tuberculosis was common. School places were barely sufficient to meet the needs of children in a city where the average age was under twenty (Hong Kong Council of Social Service, 1961).

The immigrants who arrived in Hong Kong settled into temporary and often unsanitary accommodation in areas popularly referred to as "squats". In December 1953, a fire in Shep Kip Mei, one of the city's largest squats, led the Government to introduce a change in housing policy with the construction of multi-storey settlements using public funds (Mark, 2007). However, it soon became apparent that provision of housing to the immigrants was merely the start of what needed to be done and by 1956, as widespread riots forced the Hong Kong Government to acknowledge the "problem of people" that had grown up in their midst, a policy of integration was tentatively instigated. As 'the landlord of some 300,000 refugees' (Hong Kong Government, 1957, cited in Mark, 2007, p 1150), however, the Government soon realised that, in order to pursue this policy, external help would be needed and a request was put forward to the United Nations High Commission for Refugees (UNHCR) to consider formally the Hong Kong refugee problem (Mark, 2007). At the same time, the 1956 riots drew international attention to the plight of the colony's population.

In 1956, the Adoption Ordinance was passed and domestic adoption was encouraged. A report from the Hong Kong Social Welfare Department (Quarterly Report, April–June 1962) stated that in 1959, 97 children were adopted in Hong Kong; this figure rose to 128 in 1960 and 193 in 1961.

In 1958, *Crossbow*, the magazine of the influential Oxford-based conservative Bow Group, published an article about the Hong Kong refugee situation outlining 'a plan to save the refugees' (quoted in Gatrell, 2011, p 10). This led four British politicians and journalists, including Christopher Chataway, an Olympic athlete and TV broadcaster, to propose a World Refugee Year in 1959. The British Government, acutely aware that Hong Kong was the only British colony with a "refugee problem" at the time, was quick to endorse the initiative, acting on guidance from the Hong Kong Colonial Office that this could be an opportunity for the British Government to 'restore confidence in Hong Kong' following the 1956 riots (Mark, 2007, p 1172).

On 5 December 1958, the United Nations General Assembly adopted a resolution proclaiming the 12 months from June 1959 to be World Refugee Year, which aimed to 'focus [international] interest on the refugee problem . . . encourage additional financial contributions from governments, voluntary agencies and the general public . . . [and to] encourage additional opportunities for permanent refugee solutions through voluntary repatriation, resettlement or integration' (United Nations Office of Public Information, 1959a).

Sixty countries participated in the initiative and an estimated total of US$4.5 million was donated to Hong Kong by governments, voluntary organisations and private individuals (United Nations Office of Public Information, 1959b). In 1959, UNHCR stated that the money made possible 'the realisation of projects which otherwise would have had to wait for years' (Lindt, 1959). These projects included the building of community centres, primary schools, medical facilities and reception centres for children in need of care (Mark, 2007).

In addition to raising funds for social integration initiatives in countries with a large refugee population, World Refugee Year also oversaw the opening of previously closed national borders on humanitarian grounds to adult and child international migrants. The United States had been receiving children from Hong Kong for a number of years prior to the World Refugee Year initiative, but a number of countries, such as Canada and New Zealand, which had previously had restrictions on the admission of non-white migrants, now relaxed these on humanitarian grounds, paving the way for intercountry adoption to take place (Lovelock, 2000).

In 1956, International Social Service set out some fundamental principles of intercountry adoption to ensure that good practice prevailed when children were being placed for adoption overseas. Subsequently, a European seminar was organised under the auspices of the European Office of the United Nations, and held in Leysin, Switzerland between 22 and 31 May 1960. At this seminar a set of 12 principles was formulated to underpin best practice in intercountry adoption. Known as the Leysin Principles (United Nations, 1960), they recommended that an adequate home study of the prospective adoptive parents be completed prior to the child leaving his/her country of origin (Principle 8), and that a trial period of not less than six months was needed under the supervision of a social worker from a qualified agency before the adoption of a child could be legalised (Principle 9). The overriding concerns embodied in the principles were that adoption must be in the child's best interest and that adoption was a "socio-legal process" (United Nations, 1960). There was a clear message that if one or the other was neglected, adoption would not ensure that the child's best interests were being upheld. Adoption of a child was not seen lightly, as illustrated in Principle 2, where it stated that 'sufficient considerations should be given to possible alternative plans for the child within his own country before intercountry adoption is decided upon, since there are various hazards inherent in transplanting a child from one culture to another'. It noted that such an adoption should happen only in exceptional circum-stances and ideally that there should be no need to remove a child from his or her own country and taken to another in order to give the child an opportunity to experience normal family life. As stated in the report from this seminar:

Intercountry adoption should never be accepted as a solution for a child without first giving careful attention to all possible alternatives in his own country, whether through remaining with his own relatives, through adoption, through foster home placement, or other forms of appropriate care, with the suitability of the plan being determined on a careful, individual basis. (United Nations, 1960, p 13)

In an undated ISS report, entitled *Position Paper on Intercountry Adoption in the Asian Region*, the question of identity was discussed. It reported that there was a clear indication of the problem of the adopted child "'struggling for identity" . . . especially in his adolescent stage and pre-adulthood as an Asian child in a blue-eyed blond family'.

Background to the Hong Kong Adoption Project

In 1958, a new branch of International Social Service (ISS) was opened in Hong Kong, in order to address the growing problem of abandoned refugee children. ISS Hong Kong worked in co-operation with the United States Escapee Project (USEP) to facilitate the adoption placement of children in Britain and other countries to coincide with World Refugee Year. A memorandum dated 24 July 1958 noted that the goal of this programme would be 'the emigration and adoptive placement of approximately five hundred refugee children' although it was noted that 'the number in need of adoption is very likely larger' (ISS, 1958).

Most of the children adopted through the Hong Kong Adoption Project were described as having been "abandoned". The majority had been strategically placed in a public place where they would be likely to be found quickly, such as a stairway of a residential building, outside or in a hospital, or outside or close to an orphanage. Only a few were abandoned in more isolated places.

We believe it is likely that the majority of children were given up or abandoned out of desperation due to economic hardship and the parents' position as refugees. Given the pejorative overtones of the term "abandoned", for the majority of the children in this study the phrase "abandoned to be found" would be more accurate. However, we have chosen to not repeat this awkward phrase but would affirm that for most children this is the more accurate description.

Some of the children who were abandoned had minor impairments, such as a cleft palate or squint. The ISS report on one very young baby speculated that she may have been left because she was born with two front teeth '. . . as simple Chinese people believe an infant born with teeth will grow up to destroy its mother' (ISS child record, cited in ISS UK). Once found, most children were admitted to an institution and taken to a hospital within the first day for a full medical examination. Some would have to remain for a short while before they were deemed fit to return to the institution. Others had first been admitted to hospital when found or following birth and in due course would be admitted to an institution.

In cases where there was no information available about the child's name or date of birth, their birth was registered using a date of birth estimated during their medical examination. The child's name was usually chosen by a member of staff at the institution, and sometimes an English translation of the name was given in the child's social history report, such as "a bright mind", or "tiny and strong" or "born beauty, now residing seclusively [sic] on the moon" (after a Chinese legend). A small number of names referred to the child having been found, such as "a young chance friend" or "obtained from the road". In some cases the child's surname was also chosen by a member of staff at the institution, although it was quite common for a stand- ardised surname to be given to all the children who had been admitted to the same institution in a particular year.

The public response to World Refugee Year in the UK was considerable. Following publicity in a range of media, ISS UK received a flood of enquiries from people wishing to adopt. A newsletter from the time stated that:

It was clear that many people here – as in the United States – believed that they could do something about the refugee problem by sharing their own home and happiness with less fortunate children. It is [due to] this belief that every child – irrespective of race and creed – needs to belong to a family that the scheme has grown in spite of difficulties and problems. (ISS Hong Kong, 1961)

Indeed, just three years after the opening of the ISS office in Hong Kong, with its aim to place at least 500 children internationally, the Hong Kong Council of Social Service Newsletter (1961) announced that a five-year-old Chinese orphan girl known as Little Shirley had been placed in New York by ISS, the 500th orphan from Hong Kong to be placed overseas.

Institutions and orphanages

According to an extract from the Social Welfare Department Quarterly Report, April – June 1962, in the early 1960s it was estimated that there were over 2,500 children in residential homes in Hong Kong. Most of these children were not orphans but for a variety of reasons were not able to be looked after by their parents.

The majority of the children included in the Hong Kong Adoption Project were placed and cared for in one of four main orphanages; two had church affiliations, one was a Chinese charitable association and one was governed by the Social Welfare Department of the Hong Kong government. The smallest institution cared for 65 children and the largest had capacity for 450 children. Descriptions in the records suggest that the staff:children ratio ranged from 1:8 to 1:22 (in the largest institution). The quality of care-giving varied inevitably depending on the resources available; for example, in one institution there was no room for children to learn to crawl and develop their motor skills. A lack of personalised attention from a consistent caregiver was noted in the reports.

Due to the high baby to staff ratio in some orphanages, it was not uncommon for babies to be left to feed themselves from bottles placed in their cots, or for two children to be fed at one time from the same bowl. The children's diet consisted mainly of rice, congee (a kind of rice porridge, sometimes with added vegetables or meat) and biscuits, with milk, juice or water to drink. In all of the homes it is clear that the diet did not include adequate amounts of fresh vegetables, fruit, meat or fish. However, in comparison to what is known about orphanage care in other countries at different times, there is no evidence of the most severe levels of deprivation (Gunnar *et al*, 2000).

Legal status

Children in Hong Kong who were orphaned or had been abandoned (or, in a small number of cases, were relinquished by birth parents) normally became wards of the Director of Social Welfare.

If the Director agreed that the child be placed overseas for adoption, then an application was made to the Supreme Court for the authority to consent to the child leaving Hong Kong for the purpose of adoption. If the court agreed to the application, the child left 'under the auspices of the agency in question which undertakes the duties of guardian in the country of the adoption until the final court order of the adoption is made' (Hong Kong Social Welfare Department, 1962).

Recruitment, assessment and approval of adoptive families

A number of countries responded to the calls of the Hong Kong Government and ISS for the adoption of children on humanitarian grounds. The first orphaned child from Hong Kong was adopted into the United States in 1956 following the passing of the United States Refugee Relief Act in 1953, and over the coming years a high number of children were sent to the US, where there was a growing Chinese population. Some orphaned children were placed with extended family members already living there. Between April and June 1962, 47 young children went to the US for adoption and the majority of these were placed with Chinese families.

The children who were sent to the UK via the ISS UK Hong Kong Adoption Project were placed for adoption following publicity surrounding World Refugee Year in 1959–1960; the first child was placed in 1960. The main purpose of placing these children for adoption was to fulfil their need to have families and to help reduce overcrowding and the problems in Hong Kong's orphanages with the influx of refugees from China. However, the ISS reports included in the files indicate that the organisation was well aware that intercountry adoption was not a solution to the crises at that time, but that their aim was to find families for a small number of destitute children from Hong Kong where local families could not be found.

Correspondence between ISS UK and NCH in 1960 indicates that the Hong Kong Adoption Project initially aimed to bring no more than 50 children to the UK to be placed in adoptive homes. According to the ISS files, 106 children were brought to the UK by the time the project ended in 1970. In the last two years of the scheme, as the number of children available for overseas adoption from Hong Kong dropped, applications usually were accepted only from couples that included one parent of Chinese origin, or those who had previously adopted a daughter through the same scheme.

Prospective adopters came forward as a response to publicity or after hearing about ISS from other prospective adopters, agencies dealing with adoption or projects to aid refugees. Several couples mentioned seeing television programmes or newspaper articles (particularly *The Sunday Times*) which prompted them to consider adopting a child from this part of the world.

Correspondence between ISS Hong Kong, ISS UK and the selected adoption agencies during the 1960s showed that there were clear and stringent procedures to adhere to once an application had been received. The prospective adopters were assessed for their suitability and a home study was undertaken by the recognised and designated social welfare agency where they lived. The assessment included their personal fitness to be parents and their home conditions and surroundings.

As there was some variation in the level of detail recorded in the home study, in some cases ISS UK requested further information if the initial report was not considered sufficient. For example, following one such report in 1964, ISS UK requested further information about 'the physical appearance and the personalities of the members of this family, whether or not the parents appear to be well-adjusted and their marriage a happy one, and if the children are well-integrated, whether both parents are equally anxious to have this child join them, and if the other members of the family group, i.e. relatives such as grandparents and the parents' brothers or sisters would welcome an Oriental child'.

In each case three references were taken up, with many prospective adopters giving their local clergy as one of their referees, as was usual in adoption applications at the time. References were mainly glowingly positive and highlighted prospective adopters' generosity, understanding and reliability, and clearly reflected the social attitudes of the time. For example, one reference from the clergy went to great lengths to justify an adoptive mother's previous divorce as 'very regrettable but repented of long ago and best forgotten . . . I am convinced as I can be that [they] would make ideal adoptive parents'. In another case some negative comments in a reference were followed up by a face-to-face interview with the referee concerned and another reference was sought before the couple were granted approval.

The approval to adopt was decided by the appropriate NCH or Barnardo's committee and then by the Hong Kong Adoption Project committee at ISS UK. Prospective adopters were informed when their application had been approved by both committees. Following this, the information on the prospective adopters was forwarded to ISS Hong Kong in order for the ISS caseworker, working with the orphanages, to match the adopters with a particular child. This could take several months depending on the number of children who had been approved by the Director for Social Welfare as suitable for overseas adoption. Delays were also caused by the high level of bureaucratic demands in Hong Kong, which in a number of cases led to frustration on the part of the prospective adopters. There is no record of prospective adopters visiting Hong Kong before the adoptions took place. Some regularly wrote to or telephoned ISS UK asking for updates and the response was generally that there was little that ISS

UK could do to expedite the process, although staff were sympathetic to the prospective adopters' feelings of disappointment.

The home study helped ISS UK to match the prospective adopters with a child waiting to be adopted. In accordance with the Leysin Principles, "matching" was considered important to ensure that the prospective adopters would be able to meet the child's needs. Once matched, information was sent to the prospective adopters about the child the ISS caseworker considered most suitable for their family. For a small number the adoption placement did not go ahead – usually where the prospective adopters felt they would not be able to cope with a particular child's health problems or behavioural issues – but judging from the letters on the ISS UK files, the vast majority of adoptive parents seemed delighted with the children they were matched with.

Preparing for the child's move to the UK

A small number of the children were placed in foster homes in Hong Kong for a short period in order to prepare them for the transition from institutionalised care to family life. Children in a poor medical condition were sometimes prioritised for foster care in Hong Kong as they were unable to travel until their health was good enough. Reports from foster carers in Hong Kong suggest that these were usually British families living in Hong Kong, so the children also had a chance to hear and learn a few words of English. Others remained in the orphanages; the superintendent from one home did not allow children in her care to be transferred for pre-placement fostering in Hong Kong, believing that such a move would create unnecessary upheaval and disturbance for the child.

Before the child was deemed ready to be transferred to the UK, a full social and medical report was prepared. The latter would include a record of haemoglobin levels, white blood cell count, weight and height at time of examination, and information about any surgery/ extra tests that had been carried out. If the child had a disability or had recently suffered from an illness or infection, this would also be recorded along with details of any treatment. If a child had a prominent birth mark, this was also noted so it would not alarm adoptive parents upon the child's arrival. Colds and upper respiratory infections were not uncommon. Some reports also included notes on the child's motor skills and linguistic development.

Although the reports included a section on inoculations, in all of the files this was either incomplete or left blank. In a letter to one adoptive mother, an ISS caseworker explained that the medical report included all information available to the doctor at the time of the examination, suggesting that information on inoculations the child may have received earlier were not available or reliably recorded.

The social history report, compiled by an ISS caseworker in Hong Kong, would usually include information on the following, although the level of detail varied considerably:

- when and where the child had been found;
- any moves between institutions or time spent in hospital;
- a description of the institution (name usually omitted) and living conditions, in some cases information on the child's particular ward;
- a description of the child: physical appearance, personality, behaviour, health, daily habits;
- general remarks on the child's suitability for adoption.

Some files also included an additional report on the child's development and behaviour.

Once the child had been accepted by the adoptive parents and all paperwork had been completed (including the issuing of a UK passport), ISS Hong Kong and ISS UK would co-ordinate the transfer arrangements. As the children were born (or assumed to be born) in Hong Kong, they were considered British citizens and therefore eligible for UK passports.

While the children were cared for in institutions, they were legally considered to be wards of the Director for the Department of Social Welfare in Hong Kong. Once the match had been confirmed, interim guardianship had to be transferred to the sponsoring agency in the UK by a court decree in Hong Kong. ISS UK paid all upfront costs for the children's travel arrangements, including flights and "processing" costs. The prospective adopters were encouraged to contribute as much as they could towards these, although it was emphasised that financial ability to contribute was not a criterion in assessing their suitability to adopt. Initially, ISS UK received funds from Oxfam[2] and an anonymous donor who supported the scheme to make up any shortfall in contributions from the adoptive families. Some additional funding was received from Christian Aid during the latter part of the project. ISS UK also actively sought additional funds to keep the scheme going. For example, the following advertisement appeared in *The Times* in February 1964:

> 'Abandoned in a Hong Kong Alley, 18-month-old Mei Lee ("lovely flower") needs only an air ticket to bring her to specially chosen parents in Britain. Will you give something towards the £127 required? Donations quickly please, to International Social Service . . .'

Although special flight discounts were negotiated (children under two years of age could usually travel for 10% of the adult fare), the cost of transferring the children rose significantly throughout the duration of the scheme, to a peak of £122 per air ticket[3] and a £50 processing fee per child for the last group of children on the scheme. Some families held fundraising events or received donations from relatives or members of the church congregation. Parents were discouraged from taking out loans or placing themselves at financial risk. Children travelled in groups of between two and eight and could be as young as eight months old. Escorts travelled with the children, usually one per group but in some cases two.

Advertisements like the one below were placed for volunteers and one source of volunteers was the armed forces returning to the UK on leave:

---

2 Known at the time as the Oxford Committee for Famine Relief.
3 Roughly equivalent to £1,500 at the time of writing.

> *International Social Service are requiring volunteers to take children who have been adopted[4] by families in England. A small allowance can be given and all information can be obtained from International Social Service [address included]. This is an easy task which would be of tremendous service and enable a child to travel to a new home. Telephone International Social Service with date of your departure.* (Hong Kong Council of Social Service, 1960)

In all cases the children were handed over at the airport by the escorts into the arms of their new prospective adoptive parents, under the supervision of a member of ISS UK staff. Parents were often given only a few days' notice of the child's arrival and had to make appropriate arrangements to travel to London. This was made more difficult by the fact that some of the parents did not have telephones, so any last minute changes had to be relayed through friends or neighbours who had telephones at home.

The arrival of the children at UK airports was always met with interest from the media and articles carrying photos of the new arrivals in the arms of their adoptive mothers were common in national newspapers. Much was made of the exotic names of the children who arrived. One article was entitled "Beautiful Ornament from the East for a Lancashire home", a reference to the child's Chinese name, and another entitled "A Mummy for Christmas" listed the names of the arrivals as World Beauty, Admirable Blossom, Angel from Heaven, The Moon Goddess and Certainly Bright.

To the contemporary reader, familiar with daily exchanges with people from all over the world and the commonplace nature of international travel, these articles provide a fascinating insight into the level of interest the arrival of these children would have caused in towns and villages across the country.

---

4 Although this quote refers to the children as being adopted, in actual fact they had been matched with families in order to be placed for adoption but the process was not yet completed.

Settling in the UK

Once the child had arrived in the UK, the adoptive parents were encouraged to take the child to their own GP as soon as possible. The agency that had assessed the adopters was also responsible for carrying out post-placement visits, although not all reports are available in the ISS UK files. There was an expectation that the adoptive parents and child would be visited in the first week of placement. The childcare officers sometimes reported spending time with the adoptive families listening to their concerns, particularly in the earlier stages of the placement. Many files also contain letters from the adoptive parents to staff at ISS UK both during the adoption process and after it had been completed.

Conclusion

This brief history sets the scene for what follows. Unknown origins, separation from birth parents, institutional care, disruption of routine, loss and change, opportunity and a new family life are the markers of these children's histories. Each child's experience was unique but their circumstances linked them together even if most grew up without contact with other families who had adopted children through the same project. This study has provided an opportunity to explore the life course of each participant individually and for the group as a whole. Although other lifespan development studies have been carried out, to the best of our knowledge none has followed up to middle years a representative ex-orphanage, internationally adopted sample. The historical and social context of these adoptions is important to bear in mind when considering the findings reported in the chapters that follow.

Summary

- Adoption involves many legal and ethical issues. In the case of intercountry adoption, children grow up not just in a different family but in a different country and culture with all the challenges that brings.

- Many refugee families fled from political problems and famine in Communist China into the British Crown Colony of Hong Kong, causing a huge increase in the population and also many abandoned babies and overcrowded orphanages.
- The majority of the children included in the Hong Kong Adoption Project were cared for in one of four main orphanages. The smallest institution cared for 65 children and the largest for 450 children.
- The children who were sent to the UK via International Social Service were placed for adoption following publicity surrounding World Refugee Year in 1959–1960 and the first child from Hong Kong was placed in the UK in 1960.
- Each child had a file containing a social and medical report.
- Children travelled to the UK in small groups and were met at the airport by their prospective adopters.

2 What we know from research

The outcomes of institutional care, intercountry and transracial adoption

This study of a sample of adult women of Chinese origin who spent their early lives in orphanage care, and were then internationally adopted, offers an opportunity to explore a number of important questions about human development. When the study was planned we chose to take a broad brush view of the likely adult outcomes. This review of relevant research necessarily covers a wide range of topics relevant to the study, from psychological development and physical health to identity formation and the nature of relations with the local and wider communities. There are three key areas:

1. the short-term and long-term psychological, social and physical consequences that relate specifically to the experience of group residential care in infancy followed by intercountry adoption;
2. the factors that might mitigate or exacerbate the influence of early adversity on lifespan development, including the characteristics of the adoptive family environment and subsequent life events and experiences;
3. the psychological outcomes and experience of transracial adoptive placements, ethnic identification and community relationships.

We take each area in turn and review the extent and quality of the available research evidence, the relevant methodological issues and any gaps in current knowledge.

The consequences of institutional care

The study of children who have experienced institutional care in early life has made a significant contribution to our understanding of normal and abnormal development. There are many different kinds of residential care and children may experience it at different ages and for different lengths of time. For example, important studies have been undertaken in the UK on the consequences of being raised in residential group care (children's homes). These have shown that children raised in the typical residential care of the period and followed up to adolescence and early adulthood presented with serious cognitive, social and emotional problems (e.g. Quinton and Rutter, 1988; Hodges and Tizard, 1989a). Clearly, aspects of residential care contribute to worse outcomes when compared with good quality family life, but the adverse experiences responsible for bringing the child into care are also likely to make a contribution to the outcome. In all such studies it is vital to consider the full range of factors that may be implicated in developmental progress in addition to the residential care itself. For example, the effect of toxins, poor nutrition, stress, and poor medical care during pregnancy and at the birth may all have an effect on development. The possibility of elevated genetic risk will also exist in some samples.

In recent years a series of highly important studies have been conducted on the development of infants raised in extremely poor quality residential care (orphanages). Such conditions have been found most notably in Eastern Europe particularly Romania, in Russia, South America and Africa. This often amounts to seriously depriving environments both physically and psychologically (what the English Romanian Adoptees (ERA) Study Team call 'severe global deprivation'). This is likely to include malnourishment; overcrowding; lack of individual attention, stimulation and interaction; and few possibilities for the development of attachment to a caring adult. It may also include harsh and abusive treatment and lack of medical attention. It is a challenge for research to establish which and how many of all these factors lead to what kind of effect on development (see Rutter et al, 2010).

Not all residential environments are as seriously deficient as those in Romania, however. Some environments may, for example, provide adequate physical but inadequate psychological care. Some children may have been provided with more individualised and continuous attention. The specific conditions present in the Hong Kong orphanages in the early 1960s are important to identify as the risks posed to those children who lived in them may be different from other countries and at other periods. The ISS UK records indicate that the institutional care in Hong Kong involved multiple caregivers, discontinuous relationships and lack of personalised care typical of orphanages but attention was paid to cleanliness, regular medical assessment and treatment and an adequate although restricted diet. These factors within the overall exposure may have an influence on some longer-term difficulties.

Physical health

Physical problems in internationally adopted children have been well summarised in Miller's *Handbook of International Adoption Medicine* (2005). Depending on the standards of physical and medical care in orphanages, infants can experience various degrees of malnutrition and delayed growth. Infections are common in group care with greater exposure to tuberculosis, hepatitis B and syphilis. Early puberty in girls has also been reported in some samples. It is known that because the children in our sample were selected as suitable for adoption, this probably meant that any children with major birth defects did not have adoption as a plan. However, a minority of the adopted children did have health conditions such as a cleft palate or post-polio paralysis. It has been suggested that there may be long-term consequences of maternal malnutrition such as diabetes or cardiovascular problems in later life (Barker, 2003).

Psychological development

Following inadequate early orphanage care, studies have found problems in many areas of development: language, social, emotional, motor and cognitive development, and over-activity. Research evidence comes mainly from studies of intercountry adoption in the Netherlands, the UK, the US and Canada (see Chisholm, 1998; Rutter and ERA team, 1998; Juffer and van IJzendoorn, 2005; Gunnar *et al*, 2007).

Reports from the ERA Study Team have shown that, while children can achieve significant developmental catch-up, depending on their age at adoptive placement, and in comparison with a UK infant adopted group, they experienced cognitive impairment, quasi-autistic patterns, inattention/over-activity and disinhibited attachment (Rutter and the ERA Study Team, 1998; O'Connor et al, 2000). It was concluded that psychological deficits persist in a substantial minority with early deprivation having brought about "intra-organismic change". This study continues with the children now in adolescence.

One major interest has been in the consequences of orphanage care on the development of patterns of attachment. Chisholm et al (1998), for example, showed more insecure attachment and indiscriminately friendly behaviour in children adopted from Romanian orphanages than in Canadian born and early adopted groups. Vorria et al (2003), in a study based in the Metera babies' centre in Greece, showed much higher rates of disorganised attachment in infants in residential care compared with infants living in birth families and attending day care.

It is anticipated that impairments in the development of secure selective attachments may impede later development of peer and subsequently intimate adult relationships, including those with any "born to" children. Even where there is good evidence of "catch-up", questions remain about longer-term, enduring difficulties. More specific information on the range of individual elements of orphanage care and better information on possible genetic and pre- and peri-natal hazards would facilitate a more comprehensive account of possible negative influences on development. Generally, we need a better understanding of the interaction of genetic, neurological and environmental influences on development. However, despite the current limitations in knowledge and the inevitable absence of specific information on factors such as genetic inheritance, pregnancy and parental medical histories in most retrospective studies of children from institutional care, major advances have been made in understanding and identifying the significant relevant issues that influence longer-term effects on development.

Other questions cannot be answered by childhood studies alone, namely the development of identities and of self-esteem over time. For most children, identification with and a sense of belonging to their immediate family and the community in which the family lives are very important. Observable differences may raise questions in children's minds and in the minds of others. Issues that are often personal and hidden from view such as ethnic or cultural origins or the fact of adoption may become subject to public view, questions and attitudes. These are often life-long issues that take various forms and have different degrees of significance at different periods in an individual's life. Relationships between individuals and the different communities around them are of great interest, and when people's physical appearance is noticeably different, they may be subject to varying degrees of animosity and discrimination.

Research on outcomes of international adoption

Many studies have focused on samples of children who have been internationally adopted and then compared them with matched non-adopted groups. A recently conducted meta-analysis of studies of internationally adopted infants or young children, followed up to adolescence, reported that they showed more total behaviour problems than did non-adopted adolescents but differences were small (Bimmel *et al*, 2003). They concluded that the findings are largely optimistic and that differences may be due to a small number of children with extremely adverse pre-placement histories. By contrast, a study of infants internationally adopted from a variety of developing countries into the Netherlands, where they were followed up as young adults, has shown them to be at somewhat higher risk for mental health problems than a comparison group of non-adopted peers (Tieman *et al*, 2005).

The question as to whether effects of early deprivation are long lasting in adopted children remains unresolved as results have so far proved contradictory. Various considerations are involved in making sense of outcomes for internationally adopted children. Firstly, samples may include infants who have spent all their early years in orphanage care as well as those who were cared for by their birth parents or in hospitals or other settings prior to adoption. Severity of the deprivation will vary in different samples. Unless these differences are identified, it is difficult to make sense of any outcomes. Secondly, when making comparisons with other ex-orphanage studies, it must be remembered that they mostly include both sexes although the sample in this study is all female. Having a single-sex sample is an advantage in some ways, although a comparison of development according to sex will of course be lacking. Thirdly, any assessment of outcomes must also take account of the characteristics of the adoptive environment and the country in which they would then grow up. How, for example, does the adoption of children from Hong Kong into the UK differ from that of Korean children into the US or, say, Colombian children into Denmark? And what impact does the socio-political climate, particularly race relations, have on these children and their families at different periods?

From the available research it appears unlikely that intercountry adoption per se raises the risk of problems, but that a longer time in pre-adoption group residential care, especially during the second half of the first year, increases the risk of relationship problems (avoidant or disorganised attachment) and behavioural and cognitive problems.

Adult follow-up studies

Only a very small number of studies have followed ex-orphanage samples through their adult lives (Cederblad *et al*, 1999; Bagley *et al*, 2000; Hjern *et al*, 2002; Lindblad *et al*, 2003; Tieman *et al*, 2005) and follow-ups beyond the age of 40 are extremely rare (e.g. Sigal *et al*, 2003; Perry *et al*, 2005).

Some studies have shown outcomes equivalent to the comparison groups while others have reported higher risk (e.g. suicide, anxiety and mood disorders) in the orphanage/ adopted samples. Most studies involved mixed gender samples but some adjusted for proportions of males and females rather than reporting disaggregated findings. Those that have reported differences have tended to show higher rates of mental health difficulties for men (Hjern *et al*, 2002). Storsbergen *et al* (2010) found equivalent rates of depression for adopted men and women within their sample, but the men had greater differences in scores when male and female groups were compared with their non-adopted peers.

It is likely, in those studies reporting worse outcomes, that the children were exposed to more severe early deprivation or exposed to it at different ages and for different lengths of time.

Factors influencing outcome

Early deprivation may lead to various individual outcomes because other factors also have an influence on outcome. These may include birth weight, duration of deprivation, severity of impairment, the adoptive environment, and genes that moderate the effect of psycho-social stress and psychological resilience. Ex-orphanage studies may have information on some of these from records although in the case of "abandoned" children, genetic information and birth weight records will be rare. These factors can act to diminish or worsen the effects of early disadvantage and so it is important to document events in the subsequent lives of children that are both positive and negative. The influences we concentrate on in this study are the experiences of adoption in childhood and their continuing influence over the lifespan. The positive effects of good parental care are well known as is the capacity of most children to form an attachment relationship to new carers. The bulk of adoption studies have gathered information from the adoptive parents or assessments carried out by professionals, so far less is known from the adopted person's perspective.

The study of lifespan development

Although there is a large and expanding research base on short-term effects of early adversity (that is, when follow-ups focus on development during childhood and adolescence), this study focuses on an area of great concern, namely, the psychosocial outcomes in the period regarded as mid-life. There are numerous questions. Is there a reduction in risks for poorer outcomes over time? Are there life-long difficulties? Can we be sure that any such problems are the consequence of orphanage care? Can a radical change of circumstances following institutional care, especially adoption, erase, or mostly erase, the effects of early adversity?

At whatever point in the life course the assessment of outcome is made, this will not be the complete story. A sample in their teens can be doing poorly but may show better adjustment a year later. Good adjustment can be affected by positive life events and circumstances in mid or later life – estrangement from family can be followed by reconciliation, illness by a return to health, an abusive relationship can be succeeded by a supportive one, and poor parenting by better parenting. At present, ex-orphanage studies mostly do not extend beyond early adulthood. The scientific study of lifespan development over the past decades has shown considerable progress in establishing key theories, concepts, and especially findings from longitudinal research designs, all of which are important in relation to this study, which focuses on mid-life.

Adults in their 40s and early 50s might be expected to have developed a relatively stable pattern of functioning in a number of important areas – intimate relationships, including family life and for many, employment or career – as well as their personality and social identifications. These will be underpinned by a range of competencies and vulnerabilities developed over time. For adopted people, the impact of adverse early experience is likely to be lessened by the subsequent later experience of placement in an adoptive home and the potential benefits that come from a warm, stable family environment. The Minnesota longitudinal study (Sroufe *et al*, 2005) identifies early experience as initiating a process which 'thereby frames subsequent encounters with the environment'; multiple influences work together so that early experiences are best understood for their short-term consequences that can become risk factors (p 288). Similar issues have been identified in Laub and Sampson's (2003) study of men with criminal records in the US where significant divergence in life trajectories is not accounted for by childhood experiences alone. The authors propose that 'behavioural change and stability within individuals' involves factors beyond individual traits or early experiences and argue that 'to explain longitudinal patterns of offending', data are needed on 'childhood, adolescence *and* adult experiences' (p 4, original emphasis). It is important to know whether, for the Chinese women in this study, their early privations and separations have made them more vulnerable in the face of stresses such as loss and disruption of relationships. Have they been at greater risk for physical health problems and anxiety/depression, self-esteem or personality problems than matched controls? Have later life difficulties produced a more extreme reaction in these women?

Two previous research investigations have been conducted on the Hong Kong/UK adoption cohort reported on here (Bagley and Young, 1980; Bagley *et al*, 1996/2000) but without access to the baseline data from the ISS records. There have been no further follow-ups of this cohort in later adulthood.

Transracial adoptive placements, ethnic identification and community relationships

Much of the debate about the consequences of placing a child from a minority ethnic background in a family of a different ethnic origin (usually white) has occurred since our study group of children was placed for adoption. Any conclusions about transracial placement outcomes drawn from international research should therefore be considered in the context of when the placements were made. The children in this study were placed before any special preparation was given to adoptive families about possible difficulties associated with transracial placements. Much has been written since the 1960s advising adopters on how they can anticipate and try to combat possible problems and enhance their child's positive sense of self and ethnic identity (e.g. Rule, 2006). It should also be remembered that the Chinese girls in this study were largely, but not entirely, placed in white families; a small number grew up with Anglo–Chinese couples; and there was one exception.

Opponents of transracial placements have argued that white families cannot prepare children for adverse public reactions and racial discrimination. They also assert that the children will, as they grow up, feel a sense of estrangement from the majority community and difficulty in identifying with their own ethnic group. Given the background of race politics in the UK, the independent examination of the outcomes of transracial adoption is a considerable research challenge. Research-based knowledge – as opposed to opinion – has been hard won and has by no means settled the debates. Here is a very brief summary of points to note about research into outcomes of transracial placements.

Follow-up studies have mostly been conducted in the US (e.g. Kim, 1977; McRoy *et al*, 1982; Simon and Altstein, 2000; Tan and Jordan-Arthur, 2012) and in Scandinavia (Verhulst and Verluis-den Bieman, 1995; Cederblad *et al*, 1999) and the findings may not readily be generalised to the Chinese adoption experience in the UK context.

4. Studies of transracial placements reviewed by Rushton and Minnis (1997) revealed no significant differences compared with same ethnicity placements, neither in breakdown rates nor in outcomes on traditional measures (adjustment, educational attainment, peer relations, behaviour). However, much concern has been expressed that outcome studies focus on psychological adjustment and exclude racial experiences and identity development. Lee's review (2003) of the outcome research conducted since 1990 describes the situation of transracially adopted people as paradoxical, indicating that they experience a contradiction between belonging to the culture of their adoptive family yet having the appearance of belonging to a minority ethnic group.

5. Only a small number of UK transracial follow-up studies exist. The follow-up of the children adopted through the British Adoption Project (Raynor, 1970; Jackson, 1976; Gill and Jackson, 1983) was carried out using traditional measures for educational outcomes, self-esteem and psychological adjustment. The majority of the children made a good adjustment in their adoptive family settings but the methodology and presentation of the findings, especially about racial identity, have been contested. Howe and Feast's (2000) long-term outcome study of the experience of adoption, search and reunion included a subsample of 32 transracially adopted adults. The majority of their sample (including those transracially adopted)

described having good family experiences and feeling loved by their parents. However, the transracially adopted adults were more likely to say that they felt different from their adoptive family than other adopted adults.

6. Studies carried out in the US on adolescent and young adult transracially adopted people found that many struggled with various aspects of their racial and ethnic identity (Brooks and Barth, 1999; Feigelman, 2000; Freundlich and Lieberthal, 2000). Racial and/or ethnic identities may become more important with age (Brooks and Barth, 1999; Feigelman, 2000) although more needs to be known on how this takes place at different life stages and in different contexts.

7. The existing studies are mostly restricted to follow-ups in childhood and into early adulthood and more needs to be known about consequences in adult life.

8. It is important to establish whether any raised risks are in fact due to the transracial placements themselves and not to other factors like gender, age at placement, pre-adoption history, and characteristics of the adopters and their local community.

In the current follow-up, we were interested not only in traditional measures of psychological adjustment, but in aspects like growing up in a white family, the experience of racist abuse and discrimination, and sensitivity to difference in physical appearance (Friedlander et al, 2000). We were also interested in understanding the extent to which individuals may have experienced a sense of marginalisation and/or connectedness to different communities, and personal attitudes towards intercountry adoption. Attempts reliably to record and measure some of these lifespan, adoption-related concepts are not well developed and so new questionnaires have had to be devised for this study. It will be important to explore whether there are associations between social and ethnic positioning and raised levels of mental health problems.

What is missing from transracial adoption research is evidence on the longer-term outcomes and experience. Childhood experience and the adopters' attitudes and behaviour in relation to identities and communities are of course highly important, but beyond childhood, many other influences will have an impact: the world of education and work, the choice of partner and relationships with the extended family, the choice of location and the nature of the local community, and wider aspects of the country's race relations.

The next chapter sets out the methods used in the study to examine some of these complex questions.

Summary

- Severely depriving orphanage environments have been shown to have negative effects on many aspects of physical and psychological development.
- Substantial catch-up in a good adoptive home is possible but psychological deficits may remain for a minority, especially where orphanage care has been globally depriving and where the child is exposed to such care beyond the age of around six months.
- The question as to whether effects of early deprivation are long lasting in subsequently adopted children remains unresolved as results have so far proved contradictory or evidence of mid-life outcomes is lacking.
- Follow-up research is complicated by the challenge of knowing what leads to what. Studies need to keep in mind the possible influence of experiences before and after the orphanage care, especially the characteristics of the adoptive environment, which have been little studied.
- The bulk of adoption studies have gathered information from the adoptive parents, therefore far less is known from the adopted person's perspective.
- Transracial follow-up research findings are complex and often contested. Current interest is not only in traditional measures of psychological adjustment, but in social aspects like the experience of growing up in a white family, experiencing racist abuse and discrimination, sensitivity to difference in physical appearance, and marginalisation or connectedness to different communities.

3 Aims and methods

The previous two chapters have set the scene for the present study by outlining the background and relevant research. This chapter describes the aims and methods used to collect and analyse the information. It explains how we approached these tasks, including the ethical responsibilities involved.

Aims

The aims which we addressed in this study were as follows:

- Firstly, to investigate associations between the early experience, lifespan development, and adult outcomes for a sample of women of Chinese origin, all of whom experienced orphanage care as infants in Hong Kong and were subsequently adopted into the UK.
- Secondly, where possible, to make comparisons of their outcomes with other adopted and non-adopted women born in the UK.
- Thirdly, to explore the variety of responses to the experience of intercountry transracial adoption, formation of ethnic identities and community connectedness.

In addressing these aims, we set out to test the following the scientific hypothesis:

- **That there will be an excess risk at adult follow-up in measures of psychological, social and physical well-being for these women in relation to matched adopted and non-adopted comparison groups, because of the enduring effects of stressful early experiences (orphanage care and transition to an unrelated adoptive family), lack of knowledge of family origins, and being a member of a minority ethnic group in the UK.**

This hypothesis was derived from evidence of enduring difficulties in childhood for a significant proportion of those who experienced early deprivation. We first aimed to compare outcomes with UK-born women and then to explore the links between adverse early experiences and differences in adult outcomes.

As noted in Chapter 1, the full sample for this study consisted of 100 ethnically Chinese women who had been placed in orphanage care in Hong Kong in the late 1950s and 1960s and subsequently adopted (age range of 8 months to 6 years). The special features of this sample are that they are all female, all experienced institutional group care, and all were internationally, transculturally and mainly transracially adopted into UK homes during a similar time period. As far as we are aware, this is one of the first studies to follow-up, over more than 40 years, an ex-orphanage intercountry adoption sample. There were therefore a number of different aspects of their lives that we felt were important to explore.

Ethical issues

Before the project started, we obtained approval from the Secretary of State in the Department for Children, Schools and Families (now Department for Education), which allowed us to gain access to the records held by International Social Service UK (ISS UK) (now known as Children and Families Across Borders (CFAB)), for the purposes of research. Once we had received funding to carry out a full-scale research study, we also applied for and received approval from the Research Ethics Committee at King's College, London. Obtaining ethical approval is a standard procedure with any research project such as this, so that participants gave their consent to enter the study and were guaranteed confidentiality. It gave us an opportunity at an early stage to think carefully about the potential impact that the study could have on the women we contacted. The academic consultant who was a member of the research team took responsibility for ensuring that, as the research was carried out, any concerns raised by or about participants were addressed quickly and appropriately.

We were very aware that, in making contact with potential participants "out of the blue", it was essential that they had access to comprehensive information about the study and what it would involve. We were particularly aware that some women may not have known of the existence of records relating to their adoptions. It was also important for them to be reassured that we would be sensitive to the range of reactions that they may have about being approached unexpectedly. We therefore prepared an information leaflet about the study that accompanied the letter that was sent and also directed people to the British Chinese Adoption Study (BCAS) webpage, which gave more information about the research team. The letter encouraged potential participants to contact a member of the team if they wanted an informal discussion about what the study would involve before they made a decision. Participants were informed that they could contact the Ethics Committee directly if they wished to report any issues in confidence.

Piloting the research design and tools

We wanted to ensure that the research tools would not only be user-friendly, but would also elicit all the information that we wanted to gather to meet the study's aims. We were able to recruit five women who had been adopted from overseas as a pilot group. Four were ethnically Chinese women who had been brought to England from Hong Kong in the 1960s and the fifth was UK born and transracially adopted. These women are not part of the main study. Our pilot group was invaluable as due to their assistance we were able to make some important amendments to refine the questionnaire pack and also the face-to-face interview schedule.

Our pilot group was asked to complete the questionnaire pack and to comment on whether the questions were appropriate, easy to understand and complete. They were also asked to give their views on the design and the relevance of the questions. We were particularly interested in whether the questionnaire pack was too onerous to complete.

At a later stage, our pilot group was asked to have a face-to-face interview to help us understand what worked well and where there were gaps in trying to gather information for the study. As a result, we adapted the interview schedule further to ensure that it drew out more information about the adoption experience, social affiliations, and other issues that may have been encountered by these particular women. We also included more questions about positive life events and experiences to get a balanced picture of their lives over time. All the pilot interviews were transcribed to help establish consistency and standardisation.

Locating and recruiting participants for the study

Although a small number of families had maintained contact with each other, particularly during the first few years, it emerged that many of the women in our sample had little idea that so many others had been adopted through the same programme. They were certainly not expecting to be asked to participate in a research study.

Prior to commencing the study, we already had contact details for 13 women in our cohort through a reunion that had taken place in 2000. This meant that we were able to contact these women directly to invite them to participate in the study. In all other cases, we used basic information from the records we had received from ISS UK (names of adoptive parents and siblings, official date of birth, area in which the adoptive family was living at the time of adoption) to locate the women's current whereabouts.

To trace these women, we obtained access to publicly available birth, marriage and death records and current and previous electoral rolls available online. Where a potential match was found, we cross-referenced this information alongside land registry deeds, probate records, professional networking websites, media publications and other public information as relevant. We made every effort to ensure that we had identified the right person before contacting them, including ordering a certificate (e.g. a marriage certificate) where possible to confirm this.

Where it proved impossible to trace the woman in question, we used the same methods to contact an adoptive sibling or other relative, and once contact was established with a family member, we then asked them to forward information about the study on our behalf.

In total, we located 99 of the original group of 100 women, as shown in the figure below. Sadly, we found that two women had died and one woman was unable to participate due to health reasons. Another two women initially agreed to participate in the study but in the end decided to withdraw because of changes in their personal circumstances.

Figure 3.1
British Chinese Adoption Study participant sample

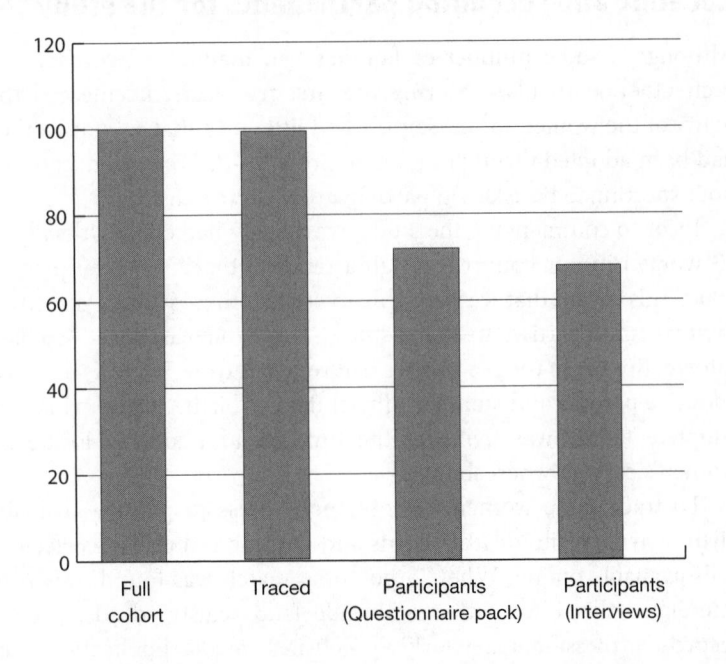

We are delighted that we received positive responses from 72 of the 94 remaining women – 77 per cent. All 72 participants completed a copy of the questionnaire pack detailed below, and we carried out semi-structured interviews with 68 of them. All interviews were carried out face-to-face, with three exceptions carried out over the phone where participants were living overseas.

Of the 22 women who were traced but chose not to participate, 13 declined directly or via a family member and we received no response to our letters from the remainder. Some women who chose not to participate asked to be kept informed of the progress of the study. We were pleased to maintain some contact with these women and to put them in contact with other similarly adopted women if they wished. One set of adoptive parents declined on their daughter's behalf because of her enduring learning and social difficulties.

The research design

Methodological approach

As has been outlined, we designed the research study to gather information through a comprehensive questionnaire pack and where participants agreed, a subsequent in-depth interview. The quantitative information (the standardised measures, demographic information, the numerical ratings from each interview) was included to help us make comparisons of these women's outcomes both within the group and with other adopted and non-adopted women. The qualitative data from the interviews (along with written comments extracted from the questionnaire packs) provided a narrative account of the women's lives in their own words.

As well as spending their early lives in Hong Kong and then being adopted by families in the UK, these women have had several decades of post-adoption life events and experiences. We considered that a mixed-methods approach was the best way to gather information on a range of different aspects and to help us understand the patterns formed across the lifespan.

Comparison groups

Although this information about the women's lives is of interest in its own right, we wanted to be able to compare this with data collected for other studies. Whatever outcomes were revealed could be due to any number of factors and it would not be possible to interpret whether being adopted from Hong Kong had contributed to these outcomes without comparison with other groups of adopted and non-adopted women.

Therefore the study was designed so that outcomes could be compared with:

1) A general population sample of non-adopted women matched for age. To achieve this we obtained access to the National Child Development Study (NCDS) 1999/2000 and 2004 sweeps for the 1958 cohort. The UK Data Archive is administered by the Economic and Social Data Service (ESDS) at the University of Essex. This large-scale UK epidemiological study began as a Perinatal Mortality Survey with data collected on all children born during one week in March 1958. This sample has been followed up regularly with relatively low losses to the sample over time. There were 5,115 respondents of non-adopted women from the original birth cohort at sweep 6. As with other national cohort studies, the NCDS had a loss to sample over time (for more information see Hawkes and Plewis, 2006). For sweep 6, the response was 71 per cent and we note that as there was greater loss for men than women, the participation rate will be higher for the two comparison groups we used. The participants are approximately the same age as the study women, whose average year of birth is 1961.

2) A sub-sample from the same database of 50 British-born women who were adopted as infants by families in the UK.

Some items were also included so that information could be related to the Adoption Search and Reunion sample (Triseliotis et al, 2005), which included a group of 81 women who participated in that study. Their average year of birth was 1963.

It would have been of great interest to have a comparison with other Chinese women. Various possibilities were considered for this purpose: these included a sample that had remained in the orphanages in childhood, or were later fostered or adopted in Hong Kong; or a group adopted entirely by Chinese families in the UK; or a group of UK-born Chinese women. As it did not prove practical to recruit any of these groups, we could not control for "growing up Chinese".

Data on early experiences

As indicated earlier, we were given access to the orphanage files that were held by ISS UK, which, in most cases, had lain untouched for many years. Our first task was to investigate the information recorded on these files.

The files provided baseline data on age at entry to, and exit from, the orphanages and therefore the length of exposure to institutional childcare for every child who had been adopted as part of this group. As discussed in Chapter 1, a range of information was also available about the circumstances in which children were found and the institutions where they had been cared for before coming to the UK. We systematically recorded important dates and other information to give us key data about each child and a comprehensive picture of life in the orphanages. The files also contained records of the routine medical check-ups on the children. In assembling the data we ascertained which items of information were available on all the children and first extracted these from a random selection of ten files. New variables were added as a result and through regular discussion and review by the team. Finally, information was extracted case by case and entered onto a database.

Given that so few studies of children who have experienced early orphanage care have access to information about the children's lives prior to adoption, the file information was an important asset. It enabled us to consider how different events in a child's early life might influence their outcomes at a later stage. Many studies rely either on adoptive parents' recollections of their trips to the orphanage or on very limited information (e.g. age at placement and country of origin). The ISS UK files contained documents from a range of sources including childcare caseworkers in Hong Kong, ISS staff in the UK and adoptive parents.

Data collection at the adult follow-up

The major sources of information at the follow up were the questionnaire pack and the face-to-face interviews.

The questionnaires

Detailed information was collected from these women using a self-administered questionnaire pack sent to the participants prior to the face-to-face interview and collected at the time of the interview. The total questionnaire pack consisted of approximately 200 items and in the event took from 50 minutes to 3.5 hours to complete. Appendix 1 provides a table listing the questionnaires that were used and the samples available to make comparisons. In some cases modified versions were used that fitted the experiences of this particular group.

We also devised new questionnaires for the study as we wanted to find out about how the participants related to Chinese and British (or both) communities and cultures, and how they felt about their Chinese appearance. Having searched for suitable existing questionnaires, we did not find any that were appropriate for this sample. In devising these questionnaires we acknowledged that people have more than one identity (gender, ethnicity, culture, nationality, occupation, class, etc.) and that identities may shift over time.

Most of the questionnaires were included in the pack but two short measures were embedded in the interviews (Malaise Inventory and Vulnerable Attachment Style Questionnaire). In addition to the standard questionnaires, information was collected through the pack on other markers of personal history, current circumstances and functioning, as follows:

- current location and family circumstances
- open communication about adoption
- leaving home
- relationship with adoptive family members over time
- partnerships, reproductive history and children
- education and employment
- psychological health and well-being
- physical health and lifestyle
- social support.

In designing the study we had to consider which areas of adult functioning were likely to bear some relationship to poor early experience. We were aware from other research into intercountry adoption that shared early experiences do not necessarily predict similar outcomes (see Chapter 2). Although we conjectured that the ability to form close personal relationships might be affected (because of the atypical early rearing experience) and the women may have experienced mood disorder and conflicts of identity, we reasoned that many other differences might be evident in other domains for some women. Our chosen strategy was therefore to take a broad-brush approach and try to cover as much psychological, physical and social territory as was practicable and was reasonable to ask of the women. We were also mindful of the ways that people are able to deal positively with adversity and so wanted to capture ways of coping with life's challenges. In addition, we had an interest in whether such a sample would be at higher risk for specific physical health problems related to their early experiences. In summary, the measures were chosen:

a) to pick up a broad span of physical and psychosocial indicators of outcome;
b) to permit comparison with matched groups of women using standard measures where possible; and
c) to have salience for this specific sample.

Semi-structured interviews

Face-to-face interviews were conducted in the women's homes (or at a chosen location) and lasted between 90 minutes and four hours. The interviews were audio-recorded (subject to the respondent's permission) and fully transcribed. Questions were included that permitted comparison with available NCDS records, namely on independent living, relationships, employment and education history and some aspects of physical and psychological health. The interviews also covered experiences that were specific to this particular group of women about their early years and being adopted into the UK. The research interviews were conducted by experienced researchers/ adoption workers with specific training in the delivery of the interview schedule. Regular discussions helped to compare interviewer experiences and to standardise the interview style.

Obtaining a life history

Childhood and adolescence in the adoptive home

We developed a series of questions that covered the women's recollections of childhood and adolescence, including experiences and relationships within the adoptive home, openness in communication about origins and difference, and feelings of belonging or being treated differently within the family and by the wider community. We also incorporated into the interview some items from previous research into experiences of care and abuse in childhood (Bifulco *et al*, 2005). These did not relate specifically to adoption but helped us to understand more about respondents' relationships during childhood, for example, to whom they would turn if a problem arose or whether they had ever suffered any maltreatment.

Adult history from age 17 (or age at leaving home, if earlier)

We selected the Adult Life Phase Interview (ALPhI) (Bifulco *et al*, 2000) as a way of tracking personal histories that moved away from a simple checklist of life events. We adapted the ALPhI to explore more specific adoption-related experiences and to find out more about the positive events and experiences in the women's lives over time. The interview covered a range of domains, including partnerships, parenthood, relationships with adoptive family members over time, friends and social relationships, employment and education, physical health and any major life changes.

Some of the questions were specific to the experiences of this group of women. We asked about how adopted people who, in most cases, have no prospect of obtaining family background information or contacting birth relatives, perceive how this has affected their lives. The interviews allowed for more open questions on identification and self-regard in order to allow participants greater elaboration on these complex topics.

Further analysis (not presented in this book) will allow us to explore in greater detail the relationship between post-adoption experiences and life events and adult outcomes following early adversity. The ALPhI is designed to record life events and phases with an emphasis on changes that mark a transition from one phase to another.

The Advisory Group

An Advisory Group was established, which included researchers, academics and representatives from agencies involved in facilitating the adoptions. The group met every six months throughout the duration of the study. It provided a forum in which to discuss relevant ethical, design and analysis queries. The expertise in the Advisory Group ensured that the design of the study and the questionnaires were appropriate in order to realise the aims of the study.

Summary

The first three chapters have summarised the background to this research by outlining what was known about the adoption programme that brought the girls to the UK, what has been learned from previous research with other samples, and the methodological approach taken for this study and the measures employed. From Chapter 4 onwards we present the analyses and findings from the questionnaire and interview data.

We had three main aims:

1) to investigate links between the early experience of orphanage care, later development and adult outcomes;
2) to make comparisons with other adopted and non-adopted women born in the UK;
3) to explore the experience of intercountry transracial adoption, formation of ethnic identity and community connectedness.

- We have outlined ethical issues, piloting the study and recruiting the sample.
- We have described our mixed-methods approach to the study and the content of the questionnaire packs and interviews.

4 A brief summary of the main findings

In this chapter we present a summary of the main findings in order to give the reader an overview of what we have discovered. Subsequent chapters offer accounts of life stages and experiences in more detail. The preceding chapter has already presented all the measures and interview schedules that we used and our comparison groups.

The children – information about entering, leaving and length of orphanage care

The children were cared for in institutions across Hong Kong. Complete information was available from the ISS files on the date of entry to the orphanage (from September 1957 to June 1968) and the date of leaving the orphanage (from September 1960 to August 1969). The average duration of orphanage care was 20 months.

Entry into orphanage care

Figure 4.1 shows the age of the young children at entry into the orphanages. The average age at entry was two months (ranging from under one month to 15 months). The largest group entered within a month of their estimated birth (n = 38), followed by those entering between one month and six months (n = 23) and a small group who entered aged older than six months (n = 11).

Leaving orphanage care

The second measure is the age of the child on leaving the orphanage and therefore equivalent to the date of the adoptive placement. The age at exit varied between 8 months and 72 months (see Figure 4.2 for a breakdown). The average was 22 months (sd 13).

Duration of orphanage care

The third measure is the duration of care in the orphanage. This was calculated based on the dates of entry and exit. Total time spent in

Figure 4.1
Age at entry into orphanage care

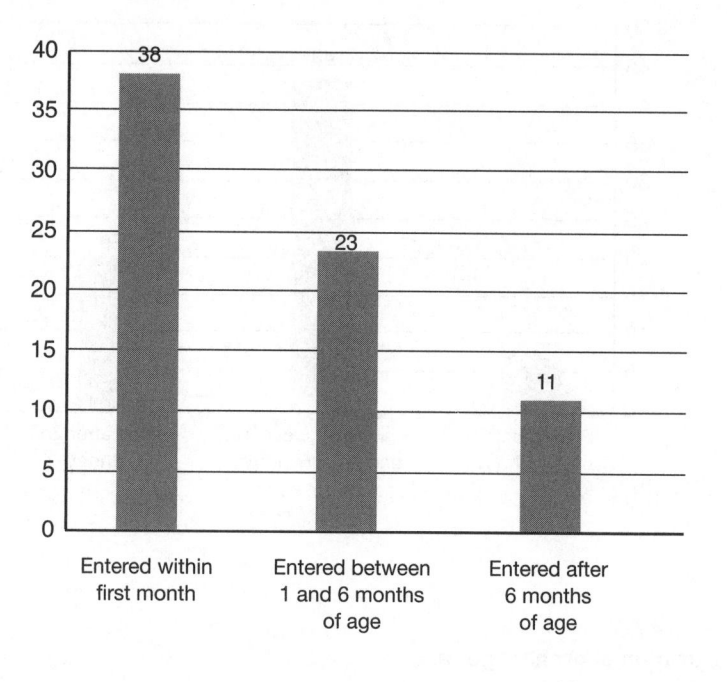

Entered within first month	Entered between 1 and 6 months of age	Entered after 6 months of age

orphanage care varied between 5 months and 82 months – that is, one child stayed nearly seven years. The mean was 20 months (sd 13). As shown in Figure 4.3, the largest group spent a period of between one and two years in orphanage care (n = 36).

In addition to time spent in the orphanages, some children spent short periods in hospital after being found, including one child who spent three months receiving treatment in hospital. At least one child had regular hospital stays for post-polio treatment throughout her time in institutional care.

Most of the files contained comprehensive information on height and weight. Just over half of the children were described as malnourished by the doctors who completed their health assessments. The majority of children had blood analyses recorded including haemoglobin levels and white blood cell counts. A low haemoglobin level

Figure 4.2
Age at exit from orphanage/placement for adoption

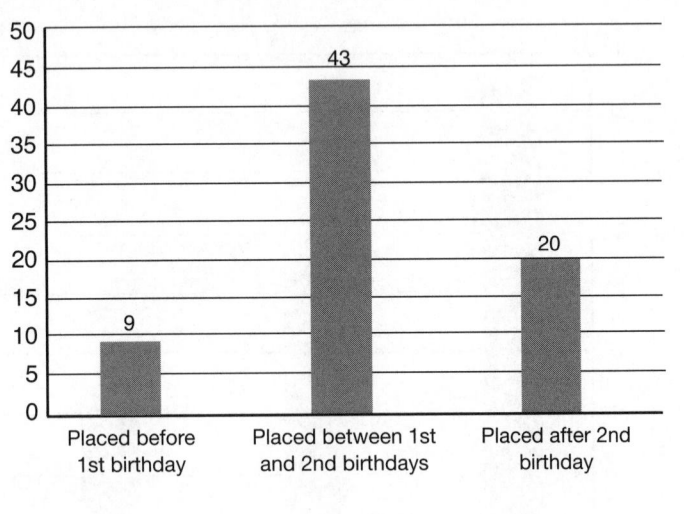

Figure 4.3
Duration of orphanage care

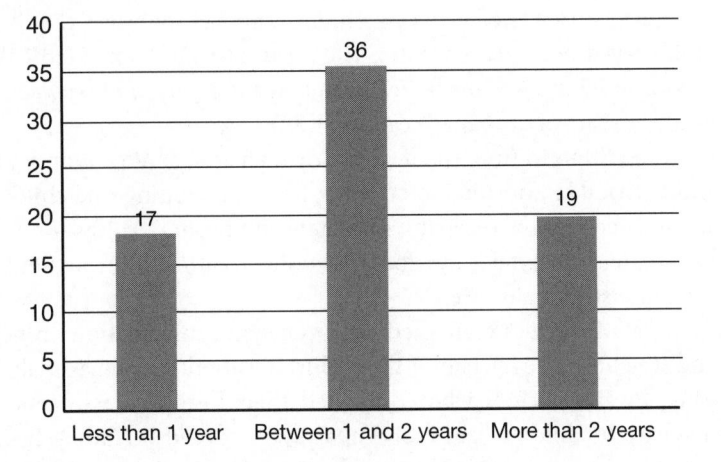

indicates anaemia, the most likely cause being iron deficiency anaemia related to poor diet. High white cell counts indicate the presence of an ongoing or underlying infection. Some children had physical disabilities recorded, both treated and untreated.

Life in the institutions – quality of care

Most of the children were admitted to four main institutions; two children were cared for in other institutions and three children's files do not give enough information to identify the institution concerned. In comparison with other studies of ex-orphanage samples, these children appear to have experienced a reasonable quality of physical and medical care and nutrition. The staff-children ratio varied between 1:8 and 1:22 across the homes and rotation of care staff meant the children will have lacked the one-to-one care and stimulation provided in ordinary parenting. However, it is possible (based on photographs and other research we have collected about life in the orphanages) that some children could have formed more meaningful relationships in these homes.

The adopters

Key information on the adopters was routinely recorded on the files. They were all married couples. The majority of the adopters were ethnically white British, although nine of the girls had one parent of Chinese or mixed Chinese/white British ethnicity. The mean age of the adoptive mothers at the date of the adoption was 33 years (sd 5.3, range 25 to 46 years); that of the adoptive fathers was 35 years (sd 5.0, range 25 to 49 years).

More than half of the adoptive mothers identified their occupation as housewife. Several had previously worked as school teachers or nurses and a minority held other roles such as factory worker or dressmaker. Very few were employed outside the household at the time of the initial application. The adoptive fathers' occupations ranged from business and professional (company managers, doctors, teachers, engineers, religious leaders) to skilled workers (carpenter, etc.).

Categorising the information from the adoption files

We turned the information consistently available on individual cases into groupings (variables) in order to carry out the quantitative analysis. Variables related to the following were used in the subsequent analyses:

Orphanage care

- name of institution
- age at entry into orphanage care (months)
- age at exit from orphanage care (months)
- malnourishment recorded in medical report.

Adoptive family configuration

- age of adoptive mother (years)
- age of adoptive father (years)
- having a Chinese parent or evidence of pre-existing links to East Asia
- adopted sibling in the family at the time of child's placement
- birth child of adopters in the family at the time of child's placement.

Checking for sample bias

The possibility of sample bias for those entering the study was checked against those who were contacted but did not participate. We found that on the above variables extracted from the orphanage records, only one (age at entry to orphanage care) showed a significant difference between participants and non-participants (participants mean = 1.96 months; non-participants mean = 5.35 months; t = 2.8, df = 94, p = .005). We are not able to suggest a reason as to why this difference might have an impact on who chose to participate as adults. However, we note that for both groups, the average age at which they entered orphanage care was at under six months and the difference between the mean group ages at entry to orphanage care was only about 15 weeks.

Comparisons between the study sample and the NCDS adopted and non-adopted women

As noted in the previous chapter, we predicted that the BCAS women, as a group, would show a higher risk at adult follow-up in psychological and physical well-being in relation to matched adopted and non-adopted comparison groups. This was based on the expectation of the enduring negative effects of early experience (separation from birth parents, lack of personalised care in the orphanage, lack of knowledge of family origins), transfer to an unrelated family where physical differences were obvious, and growing up with potentially complex questions of identities and belonging.

Our comparison measures on psychological well-being were the Malaise Inventory and the General Health Questionnaire (GHQ), Mental Health Consultation Index, and sense of control and life satisfaction measures

For the Malaise Inventory, we carried out tests for significant differences on the proportion with high scores i.e. higher problem levels (8 or above). These were found to be greater in both the NCDS groups compared with the BCAS sample. However, these differences were non-significant in both comparisons. We also tested the differences for high GHQ scores between the study sample and the comparison groups but found no significant differences. Within the Mental Health Consultation Index, depression and anxiety showed no significant differences between the groups and the incidence of help-seeking for other mental health problems was very low for all groups.

Table 4.1 shows the comparison of the study sample first with the NCDS non-adopted and then the adopted women. Differences were tested using chi-squared or t-tests for continuous variables. As this shows, our original hypothesis was not confirmed in that there were no statistically significant differences in proportions above the cut-off points between the three groups on these mental health measures.

We were also interested in the spread of scores for the women in each group on both the Malaise Inventory and the GHQ. Figures 4.4 and 4.5 show the middle 50 per cent of cases from each group in the central boxes. The two lines above and below each box indicate where the majority of cases fall (excluding any extremes). As Figures 4.4 and 4.5 indicate, there was very little difference between any of the three groups.

Table 4.1
Comparison on mental health and well-being

Outcomes	BCAS (A) (n=72) %	NCDS non-adopted (B) (n=5, 115) %	Significance p value (A vs B)	NCDS adopted (C) %	Significance p value (A vs C)
Mental health					
High score on Malaise scale (score 8 or above)	9	16	n/s	18	n/s
High score on GHQ12 (score =>12)	43	47	n/s	50	n/s
Mental Health Consultation Index					
Depressed	26	28	n/s	34	n/s
Anxious	11	9	n/s	20	n/s
Phobia	8	6	*	8	*
Mania	1	0	*	2	*
Compulsion	3	1	*	2	*
Hallucinations and delusions	3	1	*	0	*
Alcohol problem	1	1	*	2	*
Drug problem	0	0	*	0	*
Any of the above	32	32	n/s	36	n/s

* For these items, the very small proportion of positive responses in each comparison made tests for statistically significant differences invalid.

Figure 4.4
Malaise scores for the study sample and the comparison groups

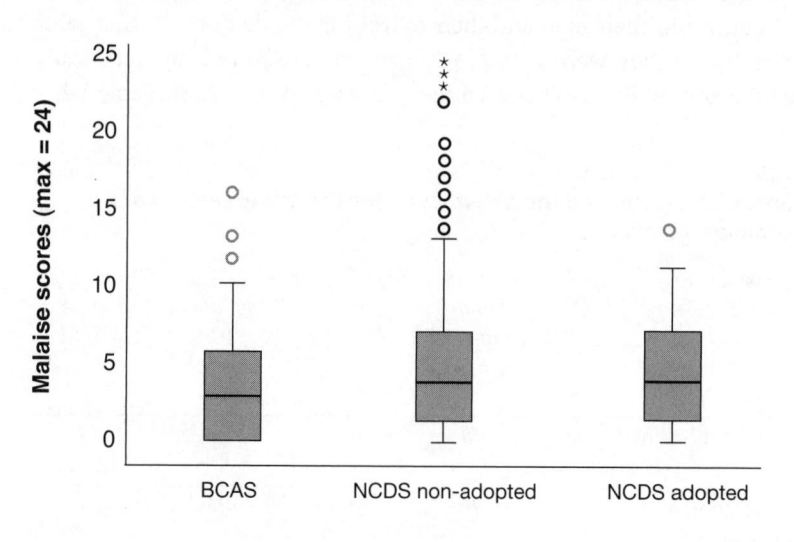

Figure 4.5
GHQ scores for the study sample and the comparison groups

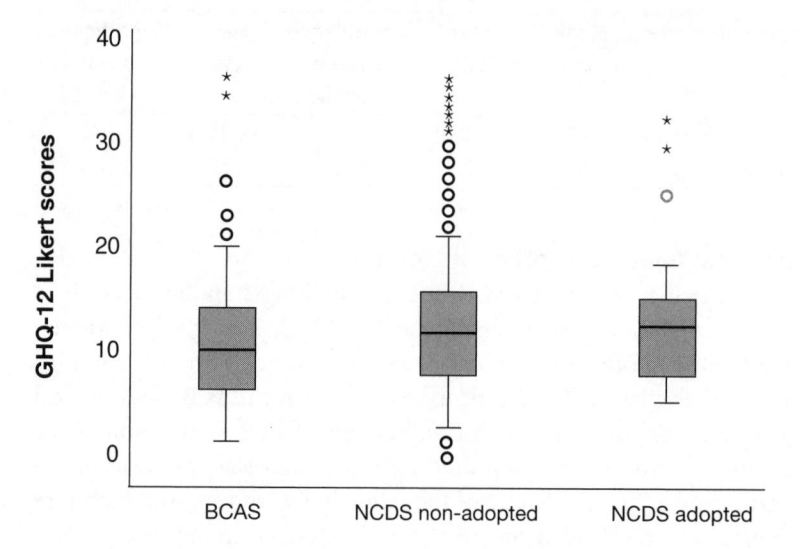

We also tested whether there were differences in the proportions of women who agreed with three statements (see Table 4.2) about sense of control in their lives and their scores on a scale of how satisfied or dissatisfied they were with life in general. We found no statistically significant differences between the groups, as displayed in Table 4.2.

Table 4.2
Sense of control and life satisfaction for the study sample and comparison groups

Sense of control	BCAS (A) (n=72) %	NCDS non-adopted (B) (n=5, 115) %	Significance p value (A vs B)	NCDS adopted (C) (n=50) %	Significance p value (A vs C)
Get what I want out of life	83	79	n/s	80	n/s
Have control over life	89	90	n/s	84	n/s
Run my life as I want to	93	94	n/s	96	n/s
Life satisfaction	**Mean (sd)**	**Mean (sd)**	**Significance p value (A vs B)**	**Mean (sd)**	**Significance p value (A vs C)**
Life satisfaction scale (0–10)	7.5 (2.0)	7.3 (2.0) 32	n/s n/s	7.5 (1.8) 36	n/s n/s

Physical health and other outcomes

The participants were asked to specify any long-standing conditions that affected them (excluding mental health). One-third of the women reported some form of difficulty, with no one condition predominating. Examples included cancer, joint pain, hepatitis B, neurological problems, asthma, allergies and other miscellaneous ailments. None of these conditions was reported by more than four per cent of the participants. The incidences of the following were very low (no more than 2%), which ruled out tests for differences among the groups:

diabetes, problems with illicit drug use, epilepsy. The current sample did not appear to have elevated health risks as a group. Some problems were the result of accidents and clearly not related to orphanage care.

The Modified Global Assessment of Functioning Scale (GAF), as described earlier, was a rating of current global functioning by research interviewers at the end of the interview. The ratings were remarkably positive: 87 per cent were judged to have superior or good functioning and the remaining 13 per cent were assessed as having some difficulties in functioning. Only one person was currently under psychiatric care for a chronic disorder.

We tested for group differences in emotional support, namely, whether the participants had someone currently they could turn to for support or other help in their personal life, and whether they could talk frankly and share their feelings with him or her. Very few people – less than three per cent – in any of the groups (BCAS, NCDS adopted and NCDS non-adopted) reported lacking this type of confidante.

Most of the results presented above have concerned comparisons across groups and, as has been shown, we found no evidence to suggest marked differences in outcomes for the study sample and the comparison groups on the items measures. This was contrary to our expectation that the study sample would be at greater risk for poorer outcomes.

Differences between the women in the study sample

This next section focuses on other areas where information was not available for the NCDS comparison groups but was of interest in relation to the BCAS women's lives. We start by reporting on outcomes including ethnic and social identifications, self-esteem and social relationships. We then examine whether early experiences before and after adoption seemed to predict differences in outcomes.

Ethnic and social identification

A detailed report on this complex topic and the implications of the findings are provided in Chapter 9. We report here some of the headline results.

The majority (68%) scored low on our scale of "connectedness to Chinese Communities". Despite having little social connection with Chinese communities, they nevertheless had an interest in language and some aspects of culture. A quarter had tried to learn Chinese (usually Mandarin or Cantonese) but few had succeeded in reading or speaking it.

The majority of the sample (72%) scored high on our scale of "connectedness to UK society". Most reported feeling a sense of belonging in Britain and were happy to be thought of as British. When asked how they identified themselves, 50 per cent said Chinese, 19 per cent said British and a further 19 per cent said British Chinese. The remaining responses sometimes indicated an identification related to time spent living overseas.

When growing up, 44 per cent of participants felt comfortable with their Chinese appearance but this figure rose to 88 per cent when asked about their current feelings. Seventy-five per cent of participants reported times when they wished they looked less Chinese when growing up, but this had reduced to 19 per cent who still experienced this at times now. Fifty-four per cent recalled feeling uncomfortable with comments about looking different from their adoptive families when they were younger. This figure reduced to 31 per cent who still feel uncomfortable as adults. We also asked whether participants currently feel uncomfortable in certain social situations in the UK because of their Chinese appearance. The majority of the sample (57%) disagreed or disagreed strongly with this.

Most of the women had been on the receiving end of racism or prejudice in some form, from extreme examples to more subtle ones that were more difficult to decipher. This ranged from being called names (at different points throughout their lives) and racial discrimination at work to, in isolated examples, being physically attacked. Not all the perpetrators were white nor did all experiences take place in the UK.

Our analysis suggests that although the majority of the women in this study did not describe themselves as having developed close links with either Chinese people in the UK or an active engagement with

Chinese cultural activities or interests, this was not associated with difficulties in psychological and social functioning at a group level.

Relationships with others

We used the Vulnerable Attachment Style Questionnaire (VASQ) to measure issues of interpersonal difficulties, namely how the women feel about themselves in relationships with others (for example, anxiety, closeness and trust).

We examined the study sample's responses alongside those of a community sample of women selected through GP surgeries in London in originally validating the scale (mean age of 40 years; range 26–59). Table 4.3 indicates higher total scores and subscale scores – which indicate greater difficulties – for the community sample compared with the study sample. Although the community comparison group were UK women of similar age, statistical tests on these differences were not conducted given the unknown differences between the samples. Whilst rates are not substantially different, there is a trend for the study sample to show lower rates of overall insecurity and dependency than the comparison groups and similar levels of insecurity/mistrust. This evidence challenges the idea that early atypical rearing may have had a negative long-term impact on adult social relationships.

Table 4.3
VASQ scores for the study sample and UK female community sample

VASQ	Median		High scorers (Above the cut-off derived from median scores from Bifulco et al, 2003)		
	BCAS (n=70)	UK female community sample* (n=58)		BCAS, (n=70)	UK female community sample* (n=58)
Total score	52	57	Cut-off >57	34	45
Insecurity	27	30	Cut-off >30	43	40
Proximity seeking	24	28	Cut-off >27	34	52

Self-esteem

We used the Rosenberg Self-Esteem Questionnaire to rate the women's positive and negative attitudes towards themselves (Rosenberg, 1965). We rated the scale from 10–40, with "low self-esteem" categorised as any score below 27 and "high self-esteem" any score above 35.

Figure 4.6
Rosenberg Self-Esteem Questionnaire scores

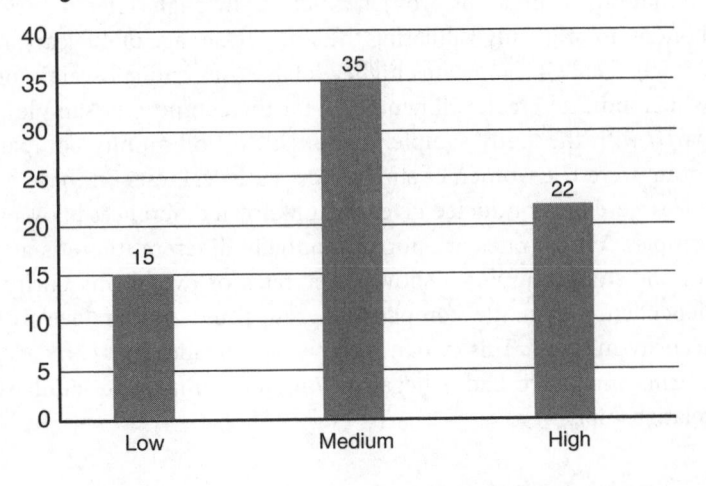

The figure above shows that those rated as having medium or high self-esteem were in the majority (n = 57; 79%). As many studies that have used this scale do not distinguish between male and female scores, it is difficult to make a same-sex comparison. However, we found no evidence of major difficulties. For example, the proportion of those rated as having low self-esteem in this study (21%) is slightly less than among the adopted men and women in the UK adoption, search and reunion study (26%) described earlier (Triseliotis *et al*, 2005; using the same sample as Howe and Feast, 2000).

Describing and characterising the outcomes

We needed to find a way to summarise a number of key aspects of the women's psychological adjustment in order to test whether this was linked to some of their early experiences. We constructed an outcome index based on the following measures: life satisfaction, self-esteem (Rosenberg), psychological distress (Malaise) and recent mental health (GHQ). After making all the scores consistent across the scales, we then combined all four measures. We called this our composite outcome index. This provided an individual score for each participant as shown in the histogram below.

Figure 4.7
Histogram of scores on composite outcome index

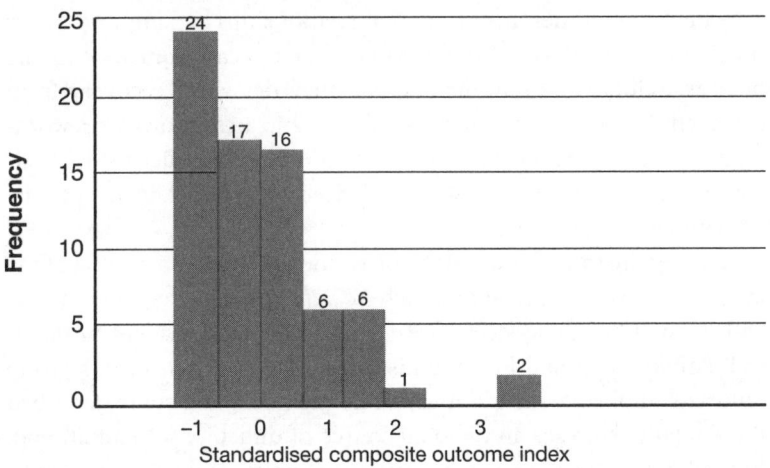

Standardised composite outcome index

To explore this further, we examined those cases that had the highest and lowest outcome scores on the index. Those women with the highest and lowest scores on the index were substantially different but with very few cases of extremely poor functioning. Among the 11 women (15%) with the highest scores (poorer functioning), 78 per cent scored above the cut-off for Malaise (7/9 women as two cases missing) and 91 per cent above the cut-off on the GHQ; 82 per cent were categorised as having low self-esteem as measured on the Rosenberg, and the mean life satisfaction score was 4.2 out of 10. By contrast, among the 11 cases with the lowest scores (better functioning) on the composite index, none scored above the cut-off for the Malaise or GHQ, none had low self-esteem, and the mean life satisfaction score was 9.2.

In contrast to many other studies of outcomes following adverse early experiences, there were almost no cases of women with repeated admissions to psychiatric facilities. None of the women had been charged with a serious criminal offence or been to prison.

Of those rated as "better functioning", most described their adult home lives as relatively stable and happy during their interviews. Not all reported their adoption experiences positively but most had found ways to resolve difficulties in relationships with adoptive family members. Sometimes this meant that relationships had improved over time, but in a few cases, women had chosen to cease contact with one or more adoptive family member(s). They described recovery from other challenges in life, such as relationship breakdowns or work-related stresses. Some had achieved considerable success in their chosen careers and none had experienced severe sustained financial difficulties.

During the interviews with those women at the opposite end of the index, they were much more likely to report more frequent contact with mental health services. Greater instability was evident in financial, employment and housing histories. More women in this group reported conflicts with adoptive family members and some described these relationships as an ongoing source of difficulty into adulthood. Poor choice of partner and fraught social and intimate relationships were frequently cited but did not apply in all cases. They were more likely to refer to a sense of abandonment or persistent sense of not belonging, but once again this was not universal within this group.

Links between early experiences and adult outcomes

Our next step was to use the variables we had developed from the adoption files described earlier to test whether there were links between early experiences and adult outcomes. We ran tests (linear regression with the composite index as the dependent variable) on the two groups of variables: those related to exposure to orphanage care and adoptive family composition. We found that neither of these groups of potential predictors was significant. Next we tested the items individually and again found that no results were statistically significant.

Early experiences and other outcomes

We also tested for links between our orphanage and adoptive family configuration variables and the scores on the VASQ measure of social relationship (using linear regression) and the mental health help-seeking index (using logistic regression). Again, we found no statistically significant associations.

As this point in the analysis none of the possible factors that we thought might predict adult outcomes proved to do so. This is in contrast to other studies that, for example, have found age at placement to be a significant predictor of later outcomes.

Recollections of adoptive family life and links to adult outcomes

Recollections of parenting

We asked the women to think about the way their adoptive parents had behaved towards them during childhood and adolescence. They were asked to rate whether they felt, for example, their parents were generally warm, understanding and accepting (using a shortened 7-item version of the Parental Bonding Instrument (PBI), subscale measuring "care"). Following Collishaw et al (2007), we used a definition of low care (defined as any score of 5 or below on this subscale (range = 0–9)) to test whether those with one or both parents categorised in this way had different adult psychological adjustment from other women in the group.

We tested for the effects of "low care" from one parent only (11 of 69 cases) as well as "low care" from both parents (14 of 65 cases) on our composite outcome index. As shown in Table 4.4 only "low care" from both adoptive parents was found to be statistically significant. This means that those women who recollected that during childhood and adolescence, both parents' behaviour towards them lacked warmth, understanding and/or acceptance, had significantly worse adult psychological adjustment.

Table 4.4
Relationship between PBI low care and adult outcome index

Mean (sd) for those reporting low care from both parents* (20%; n=14)	Mean (sd) for those **not** reporting low care from both parents (80%; n=58)	Difference in means	Confidence interval (95%)	P value
.60 (1.31)	−.16 (.85)	.76	−1.33 to −.19	0.01

*or surviving parent where one parent died during childhood

We were aware that the responses may have reflected the more authoritarian or distant parenting style of the period. We checked the responses to individual items on the scale and found that, while many of the women recalled feeling that their parents did not understand their problems and worries, 12 women, however, felt strongly rejected by one or both parents. This proportion seemed surprising given that these parents volunteered specifically to care for children known to have had a difficult start in life. Examples of different parenting styles described by the women during the interviews are reported in Chapter 5.

View of own adoption

We also explored the responses to a set of six questions relating to the women's recollections of their adoptive homes, including whether they felt they belonged and whether they loved their adoptive parents. As the scores for these items overlapped a great deal, the one with the highest correlation ('I feel happy about being adopted') was selected for testing against the composite adult outcome index. As shown below in Table 4.5, a negative or ambivalent view of one's own adoption was also a statistically significant predictor of poorer outcome.

Table 4.5
Feeling 'happy about being adopted' and adult outcome index

Mean (sd) for those who feel unhappy/ ambivalent about being adopted (20%; n=14)	Mean (sd) for those who feel happy about being adopted (80%; n=58)	Difference in means	Confidence interval (95%)	P value
.97 (1.16)	–.23 (.81)	1.2	–1.73 to –.68	0.01

Strengths and limitations of the study

In terms of the research we were fortunate to have access to precise dates of entry and exit from orphanage care and reports on conditions in the orphanages where the children had spent most of their pre-adoption lives. In contrast to other intercountry adoption samples, we know that this sample shared the same country of origin, were of the same sex, were raised in a single region prior to adoption, and had a limited range of age at placement for adoption.

We believe this to be a rare long-term follow-up to mid-life and the participation rate was relatively high. Missing data were minimal and selection bias on baseline variables did not prove to be of concern. Comprehensive data were collected via both questionnaire packs and face-to-face interviews.

Being able to compare our data with a well-respected prospective longitudinal data study (the NCDS adopted and non-adopted women) was a major advantage. Additional items were included to cover experiences specific to our sample, including direct questioning on racism, discrimination and identifications.

All studies have limitations and a relatively small follow-up sample size inevitably restricts the power to detect differences. Furthermore, some desirable information was simply not accessible, including information about genetic inheritance, pre-orphanage history and maternal health issues that may have affected the pregnancy.

We have noted before that in having a female-only sample we cannot generalise to males, particularly given that some previous studies have shown worse outcomes for men. The same applies to other groups of adopted children who do not share the characteristics of this specific sample, for example, Korean-born children adopted by American families or Sri Lankan-born children adopted by Swedish families. Neither were we able to recruit a UK-born Chinese sample.

Summary

- The children entered the orphanages early in life – between under one month and 15 months – average two months. These children spent 20 months on average in orphanage care before being adopted into UK families. They were mostly placed in adoptive homes between one and three years of age.
- The quality of physical and medical care and nutrition appears to have been adequate although rotation of care staff could not have been conducive to receiving consistent, individualised care and attention.
- When followed up in their mid-40s to early 50s, the mental health, well-being and life satisfaction outcomes of our sample were not significantly different from the NCDS comparison women. Neither was there evidence of severe difficulties in adult social relationships or poor self-esteem.
- They saw themselves as both British (by nationality) and Chinese (by genetic inheritance). The group reported a range of views on how much they took an active interest in Chinese culture and customs.
- The study did not find any associations between lack of connectedness to Chinese culture and communities and the mental health measures, but this does not discount the fact that, for some women, negotiating how being Chinese sits in relation to the rest of their life experiences has proved to be difficult.

- None of the variables representing orphanage care and adoptive family configurations were significant predictors of adult psychological adjustment. However, those who recalled their adoptive parenting as lacking warmth, understanding and/or acceptance, had significantly worse adult psychological adjustment.
- Feeling happy about being adopted was found to be significantly associated with positive psychological adjustment outcomes.
- Although our original hypothesis was not supported by these findings, we conclude that quality of the adoptive home (as retrospectively recalled by the women) and views of their own adoption are important contributors to well-being as adults.

5   Growing up adopted

What must it have been like for these very young children to have spent the best part of their lives in a Hong Kong orphanage and then put on a long haul flight to the UK, accompanied by strangers, to meet their adopters? Some of the photographs available from that time show that they travelled in their traditional Chinese jackets with identity bracelets which had their Chinese names engraved on them. They mostly travelled as a group with a carer appointed for the journey, who was usually not previously known to them. On arrival it is believed that each girl was immediately handed over to her adoptive parents, whom she would not have met before, and taken off to her new home.

This chapter explores what happened next. We report on the women's early memories of growing up within their adoptive families, with a focus on family relationships and how information about their adoption was shared and discussed over the years. In the previous chapters, we outlined the historical background and summary of the quantitative findings of outcomes at a group level. This chapter and those that follow include more details from the women's individual narratives and use quotations from their interviews and some of the comments they wrote in the questionnaire packs. All of the names used are pseudonyms to protect confidentiality.

A degree of caution is necessary when collecting and presenting information from participants when they are the only informant. The recall of important experiences and events in childhood and later life can be subject to omissions, bias and distortion (Hardt and Rutter, 2004). For example, people may reconstruct experiences to be consistent with their current mood and circumstances; their mental state at the time of the interview may lead them to under- or over-report past painful experiences and may shape their attitudes. Such considerations apply to any research that requires people to reflect on earlier experiences. However, some of the women were aware of this possibility, and did occasionally stress that recent major life events may have affected their responses. The interview style we used also involved probing for details and checking and clarifying inconsistencies, which tends to produce more valid retrospective accounts (Hardt and Rutter, 2004).

Joining their adoptive families

The average age at which the girls came to the UK was 22 months – the youngest being eight months and the oldest six years old. Although the girls may have heard some English being spoken in the orphanage, most of those who had learned to talk only spoke Cantonese. The absolute lack of familiarity with their new family and environment could not be made easier by verbal language and only the non-verbal comfort of strangers was available to them. We know from the ISS UK records that some girls appeared to settle quickly into their new families although we know little of what the subjective experience might have been. For others, there was a more explicit expression of their distress at the loss of what they had known and the strangeness of what they had come to. For example, one girl would not let her adoptive mother leave her sight and another was initially fearful when the adoptive father was present.

As described in Chapter 1, many of the adoptive parents had seen articles about the refugee crisis in Hong Kong and the resulting publicity surrounding World Refugee Year. This publicity found resonance with the humanitarian and religious beliefs of many of the couples who adopted through the Project. Around two-thirds of the adopters had cited altruistic reasons, such as wanting to give a home to a disadvantaged child, often specifically in response to the situation in Hong Kong, as their main reasons for wanting to adopt.

In contrast, Tresiliotis *et al*'s (2005) study of 93 adoptive parents of children born in the UK in a similar era found that 'around 60 per cent of adopters said they came to adoption because they wanted to create a family, with the rest wanting to enlarge it' (p 93).

The adoptive parents had been assessed by the adoption agency as being suitable to adopt, but the preparation for the potential challenges and difficulties that might arise as a result of adopting a child from overseas was different from current practice. Little, if any, professional, longer-term support was available at that time and it was not generally expected that adoptive parents would experience any problems. The adopters had been deemed capable and well able to go it alone, particularly as the majority already had children and so were considered to have sufficient parenting experience. At that time the impact on children of separation, loss and trauma was not widely known: for example, parents during that era were often banned from visiting their children in hospital; and residential care for young children was the norm rather than foster care. There was a strong belief that adopted children would adjust quickly. In adoption there was a prevailing belief that "love is enough".

Characteristics of the adoptive families

Sixty-two of the 72 women in this study (86%) were placed with adoptive families with two white British (or European) parents. Nine women were placed in families with one parent of Chinese or part-Chinese origin, and one with parents of which one was of a different ethnic background. None of the women grew up in families where both parents were from a minority ethnic background.

The information ISS UK held about the adoptive families indicates that religion played an important role for many of them, and indeed several parents cited this as contributing to their motivation to adopt: 67 adoptive mothers and 69 adoptive fathers described themselves as Christian, and in 40 families both parents belonged to the Church of England. The rest identified themselves as Methodists, Baptists and Congregational Christians. There were just four families where one or both parents described themselves as agnostic or belonging to a religion other than Christianity.[5]

Almost all of the 72 women grew up with between one and four other children in the household, with four of them growing up in

---

5   Information on religion of adoptive parents is based on data where n = 69 for adoptive mothers (3 unknown), n = 72 for adoptive fathers.

households with more than four children (see Figure 5.1). Only two of the adopted women grew up in households where they were the only child. As the majority of these adoptive parents were motivated primarily by altruism rather than for reasons of infertility, it is perhaps unsurprising that the number of siblings seems relatively high in comparison to other families adopting children from within the UK during this period.

Of the 59 women who grew up with birth children of the adoptive parents, 17 lived in households where at least one child was born following their placement. Thirty-two of the 72 participants (44%) grew up with at least one sibling who was also adopted.

Three mothers and six fathers passed away before their adopted daughter reached 18, the youngest being four years old when this happened. In two cases the adoptive fathers remarried. Three women had siblings who passed away before reaching adulthood.

Five women reported that, by the time they were 18, their adoptive parents had separated and/or divorced; in one case there was no

Figure 5.1
Numbers of siblings

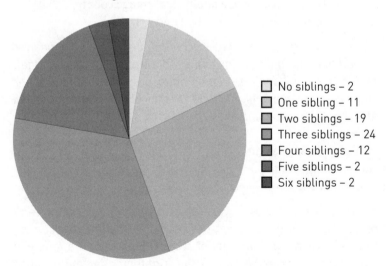

- No siblings – 2
- One sibling – 11
- Two siblings – 19
- Three siblings – 24
- Four siblings – 12
- Five siblings – 2
- Six siblings – 2

contact between the participant and her adoptive father from a young age. This is lower than the rate of parental divorce reported in the NCDS research, which was closer to 1 in 10 (Elliott and Vaitilingam, 2008).

As noted in Chapter 1, many of the adoptive mothers did not work outside the home and were largely responsible for homemaking and bringing up the children. By contrast, all the adoptive fathers were in full-time work, although some had retired during the participant's childhood or adolescence. These gender roles were reflected in the women's accounts.

Early memories and settling into family life

Many of the women told us that they could not recall coming to the UK; this is not surprising as most of them were under the age of three when they arrived. Psychologists agree that for most people few autobiographical or episodic memories of actual events occurring before the age of three are available in memory (for example, see Rubin and Schulkind, 1997). However, many of the women recounted what their parents and siblings had told them about their initial reactions to being placed with a family in a strange country.

Hayley recalls what her mother had told her:

Apparently I was like a board – I couldn't bend when I came over – I had to be taught to relax and cuddle because I was like that. And to this day I don't like being hugged by people that I either don't know or don't like. I think that probably stems from 18 months with no bonding at all to anybody. Hayley

Paula's experience was different, in that she believes that the lack of memory, along with the fact that the family she joined was ethnically diverse, made the transition less traumatic:

In some ways it was a very easy transition for me. I can't remember before [age] four, but I can only assume that coming from an orphanage with lots of faces of children to a family of other faces, it probably wasn't too frightening for me because

there were different colours and there was a whole gang of them, as opposed to perhaps being adopted as a single child into a very white family, which might have been perhaps a bit awkward. Paula

Jackie acknowledged that it must have been not just a difficult transition for herself but also for her family:

It can't have been an easy time. I know my brother has said things to me, like I was very quiet, I couldn't obviously communicate. I suppose I must have been very withdrawn for quite a long period of time. He said I used to sit in my bedroom and rock about, and nobody could get me to do anything. Jackie

Miranda was placed in a family when she was two years old. As one of her parents was Chinese, the family would try to speak to her in Cantonese:

When I first arrived, the only word they ever managed to coax out of me was Aya which means Nurse and apparently I used to stand and rattle my cot and shout Aya and that was the only word I ever spoke. Now they don't know whether that was because it was the only word I knew or was the only word I was prepared to say. Miranda

Alexandra was one of the older children to be placed (at age four) and, like the others, her only information was based on what family members told her subsequently:

I can't remember anything, but Mum said to me when she adopted me, we had a hamster and I was talking to the hamster in Cantonese. Alexandra

Leaving the orphanage, travelling to the UK, and joining an unknown family were clearly major events and turning points in these girls' lives. For the majority, it would be the first time they would encounter the intensity and intimacy of family life compared with their life in orphanage care. In the orphanages, they would have been one of many in a room full of other girls just like them. In the UK, they became the centre of attention in their new families, a focal point, and it must have been hard for some of the parents to understand why their child did not automatically respond to their offers of affection and cuddles. The family would most probably have been joyful and excited about the child's arrival and some may not have understood or known about the effects of loss and separation, and the shock, grief and trauma the child may have experienced.

Attitudes to parenting at the time the children were placed

At the time the girls were placed for adoption, attitudes to childrearing and parenting on an individual level were probably quite wide-ranging. Gender roles in the family in respect of daily care, discipline, housework and work were emerging from traditional models. There may have been a stronger expectation of the authority of parents to control their children and for children to show due respect. To some extent children were "to be seen, and not necessarily heard". In many families, although varying according to social class, "good behaviour" was a strong expectation, with parents being expected to discipline their children with an acceptance that physical chastisement would play a part. The author of one parenting guide published in 1959 wrote:

The young child is rather like a little barbarian. He is not born with any guiding principles or knowledge of what is right and what is wrong; he is guided at first by his wants and his emotions. If he is hungry and not fed, he cries – perhaps screams – until he is fed; if he sees something he wants in another person's hands, he will snatch it away. He has to be taught gradually that these ways are not the ways of the community he is growing up in. He has, in fact, to learn to be civilised. (Hudson, 1959, p 227)

Parents were told of their moral duty to uphold discipline for the good of the children. One family doctor at the time wrote:

If you deprive your children of discipline, you deprive them of the one thing that gives them a greater sense of security than anything else, and security of background probably contributes more to their happiness, meaning their peace of mind, than anything. (Hutchin, 1968, p 223)

However, good parenting guides were quick to point out that a continued emphasis on discipline should not mean a lack of love or emotional warmth. Hutchin continues:

The inability to express sensitivity can be as bad as lack of sensitivity . . . You must show your affection for [your children] and never threaten to deprive them of your love, however naughty, or even bad, they are. (p 37)

Accepted wisdom at the time meant that mothers were called to exercise discipline as much as fathers were. *Modern Parenthood,* published in 1959, advised that:

. . . many mothers shirk administering discipline or punishment. It is easier to say 'I'll tell your father' and put the responsibility onto him. This is a bad way of dealing with the problem. If you take this attitude, then you are placing your husband in a very difficult position as well as, perhaps, spoiling his relationship with the child . . . Father should not have to deal out punishment because you have been too weak-minded or tender-hearted. (Hudson, 1959, p 105)

Similarly, the father's role in bringing up children was undergoing change at this time. The widely read Dr Spock noted in the 1969 edition of *Baby and Childcare* (p 44) that fathers should not be afraid to be more involved with the care of their babies and children:

Some fathers have been brought up to think that the care of babies and children is the mother's job entirely. But a man can be a warm father and a real man at the same time.

In *How Not to Kill your Children*, the author noted a 'levelling up of the parents' position in the home' resulting in 'fathers becoming much more involved, physically and emotionally, in the upbringing of their children' (Hutchin, 1968, p 18).

Whilst discipline was seen as a moral duty to be carried out by both parents, this was to be combined with love, especially in the case of what one writer referred to as "deprived children" who were brought into the household. For parents who adopted children, Dr Spock recommended that: 'The thing that gives the adopted child the greatest security is **being** loved, wholeheartedly and naturally' (Spock, 1969, p 601).

It is important to keep this historical context in mind when reading about the experiences of the women in this study. Although some of the ISS files contained brief descriptions of the parents' behaviour towards their newly-adopted daughters, we do not know how much they may have been influenced by the manuals or instructions available at the time. But we do know that the context of parenting and expectations of family life were different and this is likely to have played a significant part in the experiences of the adopters and their children, both in relation to parenting generally and adoption in particular.

Apart from the importance of discipline, the strongest belief to influence parenting was that "love was enough". There were undoubt- edly many advances in the understanding of child development, some of which were strongly embedded in psychoanalysis, although that was also radically challenged by behaviourism. What was also beginning to emerge through the work of John Bowlby (1951, 1969) was the concept of attachment, a concept that has come to dominate our understanding of early child development over the last five decades. Central to this was a deeper understanding of the role of "maternal sensitivity" in managing the young child's experience of and reaction to separation and loss, both in ordinary family life but more particularly under more unusual conditions – one of which would be institutional care. We now know considerably more about how children make adjustments in their emotional structures to accommodate the deprivation of sensitive, attuned maternal care, particularly in becoming anxious or resistant to maternal care when it is made available. These issues can be especially difficult for parents if their expectation is that love is enough when, from the young child's reaction to this expressed love, it appears that the child cannot or does not respond. Although understanding of this was developing among professionals, it is very unlikely that the adopters of our sample group would have had access to these emerging issues, and it would have been their own resilience and determination that would have seen them through, along with support from family members and others in their community.

Feelings of being loved by adoptive parents in childhood

One of the areas explored in both the face-to-face interviews and the questionnaires was the women's relationship with their adoptive parents throughout their childhood – how much they had felt loved by their adoptive mothers and fathers.

Tables 5.1 and 5.2 summarise the degree to which the women in the study reported that they had felt loved or not by their parents. These figures are very similar to those in the Howe and Feast study (2000), which reported that 77 per cent felt loved by their adoptive mother and 83 per cent by their adoptive father.

Table 5.1
Felt loved by adoptive mother[6]

I felt loved by my adoptive mother	Number of women
Strongly agree	39 (54%)
Agree	14 (19%)
Uncertain	6 (8%)
Disagree	5 (7%)
Strongly disagree	7 (10%)

---

6   One missing case due to early parental death.

Table 5.2
Felt loved by adoptive father

I felt loved by my adoptive father	Number of women
Strongly agree	43 (60%)
Agree	18 (25%)
Uncertain	6 (8%)
Disagree	2 (3%)
Strongly disagree	3 (4%)

In looking at *both* sets of responses, 53 women (74%) agreed or strongly agreed that they felt loved by both parents; three women were uncertain about both parents and five women disagreed or strongly disagreed that they had felt loved by either parent. The remaining 11 responses were mixed, with a tendency towards more positive reports of adoptive fathers, for example, three women who felt loved by their adoptive fathers were uncertain about their adoptive mothers.

Relationship with adoptive parents in childhood and adolescence

It is to be expected that any parent–child relationship is likely to become more complicated in adolescence as the striving for independence and a more fundamental sense of being separate comes to the fore. This applies to both biological and non-biological parenting and we now know that adoption, as with many other experiences, may add a new dimension and other dilemmas to this stage. It is not surprising, therefore, to hear that a greater number of participants said they found their relationships with their adoptive mother and father under more strain in adolescence than in childhood.

As shown below, 53 women said they got on well with their adoptive mothers, and 59 with their adoptive fathers, most of the time in childhood, whilst in adolescence, 35 women said they got on well with their adoptive mothers most of the time, and 47 with their adoptive fathers.

Figure 5.2
Relationship with adoptive mother in childhood and adolescence

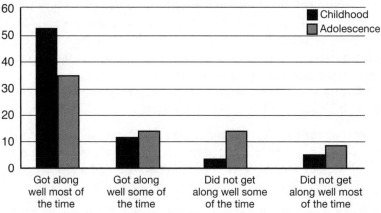

*n = 72 childhood, n = 68 adolescence (2 n/a – adoptive mother passed away before reaching adolescence, 2 missing)

Figure 5.3
Relationship with adoptive father in childhood and adolescence

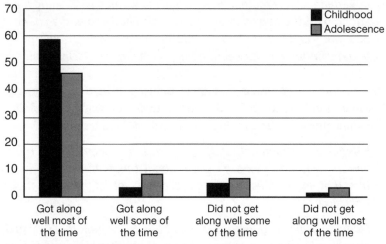

**n = 69 childhood (2 adoptive fathers passed away or left home in early childhood, 1 missing), n = 65 (5 adoptive fathers passed away or left home before adolescence, 2 missing)

Parenting styles

The majority of the women in the study recounted childhoods where they felt that the parenting they had received was sensitive and caring and that the adoptive parents generally understood them well. There were, however, exceptions to this. This section examines the full range of parenting styles that the women reported.

Erica and Josephine were both particularly positive in recalling their childhoods in their respective families:

We had the happiest childhood ever which, by today's standards, involved an awful lot of freedom; very little in the way of material things, but very high on unconditional love and just a carefree childhood. About as good as it gets really. Erica

It was very relaxed and open in my childhood. It was very happy. It was very free. My mother was very carefree and we were brought up in quite rural surroundings. It didn't matter if we wrote on the walls. It didn't matter if we made a mess. There were lots of children around and so it was very, very bohemian . . . My mother was the sort of woman who would have adopted all the babies in the world if she had had half a chance. She was really very child orientated. Very practical and loving and my father was very easy going, so laid back . . . Josephine

Many women recounted that their upbringing had been "strict", "formal" and "structured" and involved them "knowing their place". For some this was seen as being caring and just "old fashioned":

I suppose I thought that they were strict because my mum always seemed to be a bit cross about things but people were like that in the 60s, parents were very strict, weren't they? Lorraine

I would say it was quite disciplined but I don't think that was just my parents. I am not going to knock them at all. My father was very strict and my sister suffered from that as well because he just wasn't used to people going off and doing normal things. I

wouldn't say there was tension; it was just the way he thought he was bringing us up. Angela

Some women experienced childhoods that were not just formal, but also where they felt that there was a lot of tension and where parenting was described as "remote" and "cold". Faith recounted:

It was very formal. I would not have said it was relaxed. I was relaxed when I was on my own in my room. It was very structured. There were specific times you were expected to be in the living room. It was very structured because of school as well, certainly in secondary school. It did not leave you any time to have spare time because you got home, you barely had time to get changed, clean your shoes or whatever it was, then there was supper. Then you had to go and do your homework otherwise you would not get it done in time, because you had to go to bed. For several years I remember, that was all it was . . . it was go home, eat, do your homework and go to bed. So it was very structured and I was not allowed to stay up specially to watch anything. You did not really speak until you were spoken to. Faith

Earlier in this chapter we discussed how the views about an optimal parenting style were different from that of today and this was very much reflected in the accounts we received from the women. Disciplining the child and the use of corporal punishment was accepted as the norm even if its use in individual families was very varied. For participants who experienced this, it was usually seen as not being markedly different from their friends' families:

We got caned, we got strapped and stuff but that was accepted behaviour. That was no more so and no less than any other kid that I knew given the fact that caning and the slippering at home were accepted forms of discipline. Victoria

While various forms of corporal punishment were seen as acceptable at the time, there were isolated examples of behaviour which today would be considered to be abuse and where the aim was not only to assert parental authority but also to inflict hurt and pain. Child abuse was a barely recognised concept during most of the girls' lives.

One participant was brought up in a household where extreme corporal punishment was administered not only to her but also to her siblings. She recalled one of her siblings having talked to her about this:

> He asked me once when I was about 17, how did I feel about the way my mother abused me, because she physically spanked me, she gave me hidings. I am going to cry now . . . She used to get hold of me, and hold me upright and spank me. Because if she did not hold me upright, I would fall over because she hit me so hard. My stability was really poor because of [a problem with] my leg. She would hold me – like five or six whacks on the back of my legs and I have got scar tissue down one of them. My brother was absolutely horrified and this always happened when my father was out of the house.

A few of the women not only experienced living in households where tensions were high but also where there were unpredictable and sometimes extreme and unacceptable forms of punishment. One woman described her adoptive mother as a "rage-aholic". Julie also recalled a volatile atmosphere whenever her mother lost her temper:

> She couldn't half spank you, 'cos those were the days when you did get a spanking and I don't mean child abuse spanking, but certainly got a wallop on your bottom, and yes, she was quite unpredictable. Sometimes you'd think, oh, I've done something really awful and you dread it and it would be fine; other times suddenly you'd be in world war two and you didn't know how you got there. Julie

Recollections of parenting

As described in Chapter 4, we used a measure called the Parental Bonding Instrument (PBI) to explore the women's recollections of their parents' behaviour towards them during childhood and adolescence, and to what extent they agreed or disagreed with a series of questions about whether, for example, they felt their parents had been warm, understanding and accepting. We reported earlier that, in using a subscale based on this measure, we found "low care" to be associated with adult psychological adjustment. Table 5.3 shows further information about the responses women gave to the individual items on this scale.

In 65 cases the PBI was completed for both parents and in four additional cases for one parent only. The remainder did not respond, sometimes because their parent had died during childhood. The responses indicate that most women recalled their parents' behaviour towards them in generally favourable terms. Among the exceptions to this, emotional coldness and apparent lack of understanding from parents were more commonly reported rather than outright rejection.

There are various ways of looking at this. As noted in Chapter 4, these results may reflect authoritarian or distant parenting styles more common in the 1960s. In addition, some reports of negative parenting may be responses to difficult behaviour in the child. However, as shown in the examples in this chapter, some interviews included details of more extreme punitive and denigrating behaviour that would not appear to be explained by these possible reasons.

Relationships with siblings during childhood and adolescence

As stated earlier, only two of the 72 women grew up in households where they were the only child. The rest grew up in households with between one and six siblings, although not all the siblings were present for the whole of the participants' childhood. Siblings in this section refer to all children in the household, whether birth children of the adoptive parents, other adopted children, foster children or stepchildren of one of the adoptive parents.

We asked questions about the relationships the women had with their siblings. Again, there was a range of responses and experiences.

81

Table 5.3
Parental Bonding Instrument – responses to individual items

	Very likely %	Moderately likely %	Moderately unlikely %	Very unlikely %
Adoptive mother				
Let me do things I liked doing	31	37	15	17
Seemed emotionally cold to me	15	12	21	52
Appeared to understand my problems and worries	18	31	24	27
Liked me to make my own decisions	30	33	18	19
Made me feel I wasn't wanted	8	8	13	71
Tried to make me dependent on her	60	19	12	9
Was overprotective of me	51	25	13	10
Adoptive father				
Let me do things I liked doing	42	45	10	3
Seemed emotionally cold to me	3	19	15	63
Appeared to understand my problems and worries	14	30	28	28
Liked me to make my own decisions	33	46	15	6
Made me feel I wasn't wanted	3	6	9	82
Tried to make me dependent on him	74	15	6	5
Was overprotective of me	57	22	13	8

Percentages based on mother n = 67; father n = 67. Missing data due to parental death or non-completion.

Some described having had good relationships with their siblings, feeling close and feeling "protected" by them, whilst others felt more like they were the only child in the sense that they were never close to their siblings. However, for the most part, women described getting on well most of the time with their siblings in childhood (56 women) and adolescence (44 women), as demonstrated in the table below.

Figure 5.4
Relationship with adoptive siblings in childhood and adolescence

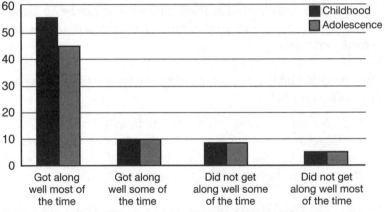

*n = 67 (missing data = 2 only children; 3 unable to classify)

Three women stated that they were unable to classify their sibling relationships, mainly because this was different with different siblings. For example, Faith wrote about the different relationships she had with her brother and sister. She described generally getting along well with her sister when they were young and as adults. Her relationship with her brother had involved more tension and this has not changed much over time. However, she emphasised that in her view the relationship would have been similar whether she was adopted or not. There were several other examples where women specifically raised this point: sibling relationships are based on many factors and adoption may or may not be salient.

83

Audrey was also keen to point out that her relationships with her siblings were not defined by the fact that she was adopted:

I have a closer relationship with my sisters than my brothers. I would say that any "difficulties" between us are more to do with family issues rather than as a result of me being adopted.

Anita said that in fact being adopted may have been a positive aspect of her relationship with her sister:

There was only seven months between us so we have been more like good friends. I used to think it was better not being blood-related as we were very different and didn't have any sisterly rivalry or anything.

Pippa describes taking on a more caring role for her sister due to her sister's medical condition:

My sister was severely mentally handicapped so it wasn't a normal sibling relationship; she also had very bad epilepsy so needed special treatments. As a child I had more of a caring attitude to her, rather than as someone to play with.

Although Patricia did have siblings, they were quite a bit older than her, so in her childhood and adolescence she felt very much as an only child:

They were quite [a lot] older than I, so when they were adolescents, I was just a young child. When I grew older, they had already left the house.

Others described themselves as having nothing much in common and never developing a close relationship with their siblings.

Our relationship was always fraught. We never bonded as children and I always felt that my brothers were always my mother's favourite and I was always told I was my father's favourite and that led to jealousy and rivalry. Irene

Relationship with extended family members

Sixty of the 72 women said they had some relationship with their extended adoptive family when growing up, although some stressed that this relationship did not play a large part in their lives. Many recalled their grandparents, aunts or uncles fondly and described them as valued sources of support or fun during childhood. Some relationships continued to be close into adulthood.

Overall, 58 of the 60 women who were able to comment on how well they got on with their extended family said they got along well most or some of the time in childhood, and 54 said they got along well most or some of the time in adolescence.[7] Fifty-one women reported that the extended family had not treated them differently compared with their adoptive siblings; 14 women that their extended family had treated them differently; and six women did not know if this was the case.[8]

In some cases this different treatment was favourable, for example, Joan said:

My father's mother was very proud of me. I remember being quite spoilt by her when I stayed and by her friends. My mother's mother saw me as a bit of a "novelty". Joan

However, other women recounted ways that their extended adoptive family's treatment of them had been different in more negative ways:

I was treated as "the black sheep of the family". At a family reunion I was once "mistaken" as one of the waitresses. Victoria.

I remember my grandmother saying she had six grandchildren plus me. Cheryl

---

7 Information on relationship with extended adoptive family in childhood and adolescence is based on data where n = 60 (12 missing due to little or no relationship with extended adoptive family).
8 Information on being treated differently by extended adoptive family in childhood and adolescence is based on data where n = 71 (1 missing).

Talking and telling about adoption

The importance of children being told about their adoptive status and having information about their origins is now widely understood and accepted. However, for some adoptive parents, explaining the adoption story can present many challenges, particularly when they fear that the information or lack of it may cause their son or daughter distress and pain. Getting the balance right is not always easy.

Although current practice recognises the importance of these issues, the advice available to adoptive parents at that time was mixed. In 1976, Kornitzer suggested that adoption should be used with babies as a 'term of endearment . . . as a rhythm, as a sound, with loving overtones' (p121). As the child grows, she advised that adoptive parents tell a story that focuses on 'mothers and fathers who wanted a baby and never had one, and how in the end they heard about some babies who had no fathers and mothers, and chose one of them to come home with them and to be their own for ever'. She adds that 'the child will be told or will guess with great pleasure that the story is really about him'.

Other approaches were less supportive. Weider (1978, p 175, p 179) concluded that:

> In the adoptees I have studied, their development and relationships to the adoptive mothers were clinically indistinguishable from blood kin children up to the time they were told of their adoption. After the disclosure, the children's behaviour, thought contents and relationships showed dramatic changes...a toddler doesn't need to know he is adopted; he needs to know he belongs.

Ansfield (1971) took an even more extreme position in which he advocated that children should not be told at all because 'the knowledge will hurt them' (p 36). He further stipulated that a position should be agreed in the family to maintain the secret by telling older siblings that 'the family is playing a game, and that no one is ever to know the secret, including the adopted child' (p 42).

Lastly, one leaflet for adoptive parents published by the Standing Conference of Societies Registered for Adoption (1950) gave the following advice to adoptive parents:

... provided that the child has not grown up with the idea that his adoptive parents do not love him, or that there is some mystery about his origins, he will not dwell unduly on these matters or want to get in touch with his natural parents.

We have only limited information about how any of this might have influenced the adoptive families in our study. One thing is very clear – in most of the families the physical differences between the adopters and their child were too obvious to "pass off" their child as a "born to child". This would have had to be addressed in some way. But the options for doing so would have been, and still are very wide-ranging, from 'it doesn't matter, we love you and that's all that counts' to a more open acknowledgement of how strange this might feel coupled with an ability to openly listen to what their child might have to say and how this might change over time. The concept of "communicative openness" (Brodzinsky, 2005) has been particularly important in focusing on how all those affected by adoption are best supported when there is a sensitive emotional openness to the facts and feelings around adoption and that this can be frankly discussed, including those thoughts and feelings which are uncomfortable and distressing.

In the case of the women in this study, all were of a different ethnicity from at least one of their adoptive parents and therefore avoiding the issue entirely was generally not an option. Forty-six women in this study (almost two-thirds, at 64%) said that they had always known that they were adopted, whilst an additional seven said they had been told while under the age of five.[9]

Being brought up in a family with a Chinese parent meant that information was sometimes shared at a later stage; five of these women recalled having been told about their adoption when over the age of

---

9 Percentages for age told about adoption are based on data where n = 70 (two missing).

five, compared with only two of the women adopted into white British or white European families.

For Jean, her parents' ethnicity had a direct effect on her view of being adopted:

To be quite honest, it was very rarely spoken about, more than anything because I didn't feel adopted . . . I had a Chinese adoptive mother so it wasn't a thing that when you went out on the streets people said how come you've got two English parents and you're Chinese, so it wasn't so noticeable . . . But if it was spoken about, I was quite happy to talk about it because it's a good thing that my parents did so, it was nothing to hide.

Emily had a very different experience, due to her parents' reluctance to let others know that she was adopted:

I remember being ten or eleven, maybe even younger than that, and that I'd go around telling everybody and she [adoptive mother] would be absolutely pissed off with me because she'd say, 'Why do you tell everyone?' and I'd say, 'Well, because it's true, isn't it?' So I'd get punished for it because she didn't want people to know.

In families where information was shared more freely, this often happened in stages and in keeping with the child's age so there was no single moment of discovery or surprise.

My parents were always very open and they disclosed the information gradually and very appropriately as I grew up. I always remember knowing the word "adopted" even probably before I understood fully what it really meant. I would say, 'Oh, I'm adopted,' but I didn't really know what I meant. Helen

Was adoption information openly discussed?

As presented above, at the time that the girls were placed for adoption, the prevailing wisdom was very much that adopted children would not experience curiosity or the need to find their birth parents if they felt loved. Subsequent research has shown that this is not the case. Today very different advice is given to adoptive parents in the UK, where they are expected and encouraged to have a more open dialogue about adoption.

Despite the commonly accepted advice of the time, almost three-quarters of the women in this study (52 women or 72%) said that their adoption was discussed openly with them.[10] In comparison, in Howe and Feast's (2000) *Adoption, Search and Reunion* study, adopted people (both men and women) of around the same age as the present sample, reported that 40 per cent of those who had searched for information said the adoption was discussed openly.[11] This relative openness within the families in the current study could have been due to the specific nature of these intercountry adoptions, and the difference in ethnicity between child and parent/s. Furthermore, in the present study, 44 women (61%) described feeling comfortable talking to their parents about their adoption and origins; 12 (14%) said they felt comfortable some of the time; and 17 (24%) said they did not feel comfortable. This latter proportion is similar to the 29 per cent of participants in the *Adoption, Search and Reunion* study who felt this way (Howe and Feast, 2000).[12]

Those who did not feel comfortable asking their parents for information about their adoption, described feeling "awkward" or as if there was an unspoken agreement that the subject should not be broached. When some girls had asked questions, responses had been minimal and they became increasingly reluctant to bring up the topic

---

10 Percentages relating to openness in discussing adoption are based on data where n = 72 (0 missing).
11 Percentages are based on data where searchers n = 392 (2 missing), non-searchers n = 76 (2 missing).
12 Percentages are based on data where searchers n = 390 (4 missing), non-searchers n = 73 (5 missing).

as they grew into adolescence and adulthood. Others, like Patricia, found the opposite. Although she felt "guilty" about asking questions when she was younger, a trip to Hong Kong in her twenties became an opportunity for more open conversations with her parents.

However, the majority of the women in this study testified to the openness with which adoption was discussed within the family. Many described it as a topic that came up naturally at different points over the years, while others felt that, while they did not discuss it regularly, their parents had always been willing to engage in those conversations as they arose.

> *Certainly in teenage years we talked a lot. I had all that inform-*
> *ation. My mum and me, you know, we read through it together*
> *and also discussed it, on and off. As an adult, when more settled,*
> *she just gave me all the documents to look after myself, so that*
> *I've got everything.* Helen

Twelve women (17%) said that the adoption was sometimes discussed openly whilst eight women (11%) reported that it was not.

> *When I first started enquiring about it, I was physically repri-*
> *manded for doing so . As far as I was concerned it was a reason-*
> *able question. From that point on the relationship between me*
> *and my adoptive mother basically started to break down. Every*
> *time I asked a question, as the years went by and I become*
> *more self-aware, it was taken as a personal affront. I wanted to*
> *learn Chinese. I was told that if I tried to enquire, the Chinese*
> *Embassy would come and try to find me and basically abduct me*
> *and take me back to China.* Victoria

Even when adoptive parents were open about the adoption, it did not necessarily mean that the child would want to know more or engage in any sort of discussion about it. Levels of curiosity differed and not every girl wanted to have adoption discussed with them. As Erica explained:

> *They* [her adoptive parents] *were very open. I chose not to ask/*

explore in more detail. In time this became the norm, people around me became conditioned to not raising the subject.

For many women, this curiosity – or lack of curiosity – continued into adulthood, as will be discussed in Chapter 7.

Telling the child about the adoption story

Overall, three-quarters of the women in our study (55 women; 76%) felt that their adoptive parents had provided them with all the information they had about their adoption; 12 women (17%) said they felt their adoptive parents had not provided all the information they had; and five women (7%) said they did not know whether this was the case or not.

Three women said that they felt they had been given no information about the circumstances of their adoption; of these, two were beyond the age of ten before being told they had been adopted and one had not been told that she was adopted, during childhood. In contrast, 78 per cent of those who had always known they were adopted said they felt their parents gave them a "fair amount" or a "lot of information" about their adoption.[13]

From the women's accounts, adoptive parents chose different ways to share the information they had about why their daughter had been placed for adoption. It is not an easy task to tell a child that they were abandoned and it needs considerable sensitivity. Josephine and Georgina both had clear memories of the way their respective parents approached this.

Josephine was told that her birth parents had left her on a doorstep where they knew she would be found, because it was a very difficult time when lots of families were so poor that they could not afford food. She was taken by the police to a children's home, where the staff took care of babies and 'knew about all these lovely parents in England,

---

13 Percentages relating to the amount of information given about the circumstances of the adoption are based on data where n = 71 (1 = "other – information given gradually across childhood").

and other countries, who were desperate to have children'. She explained:

> [My adoptive parents] *had a very simplistic story that I knew from the time I can remember so I was cushioned from all the questions that inevitably would come to you. 'Why don't you look like your parents? How did you get here? Why don't you speak Chinese?' I had the information there which makes it a lot easier.*

Georgina told us:

> *I remember about how my parents would do it . . . it's a way that I would recommend. They told me when I was too young to fully understand what they were saying – the last recollection I have of it. I would be at the end of my bed and Mum would snuggle up next to me, and she'd say something to me like, 'Now you do remember how we got you, don't you?' And I remember saying to her, 'Yeah I know that, that's boring, tell me a proper story!'* (laughter). *Repetition is important with little children so I can see I got to the point where I was like, yeah, I know, come on, can we move on?'*

Other women were told just the basic facts about why they had been adopted without the information being cushioned in any way, or recalled that their parents very rarely broached the subject.

Nicola's experience was unusual in its cruelty. She had been found in a box when she was eight months old, well fed and clothed. She recalled her adoptive mother telling her that the fact that she was not a newborn when she was abandoned meant that her own behaviour as a baby was the reason her birth mother had given her up. This had a lasting effect on her own views:

> *If [it] had just been, 'don't want a girl, want a boy' I would have been got rid of straight away. There was this eight months thing so my mother always told me that I was so bad that my own mother could only put up with me for eight months.*

And to be honest, I kind of think there is actually a truth there.

Whilst over three-quarters of the women in this study (76%) said that they believed that their adoptive parents had given them all the information they had, a small number found out later that some of the information given was not true, as in the case of Marylyn:

When I was growing up I was always told that I was given up to an orphanage. Later, as an adult, I found my original birth certificate which said I was abandoned on a road. I asked my mother did she know this and she said yes.

The above accounts illustrate that the women had a range of experiences about how their particular adoption story was relayed to them, how openly the adoption was discussed, and how comfortable they felt about asking questions. For some, the memories of how this information was shared had been imprinted on their minds, whether conveyed in a negative or positive way. For others, their adoptive status became part of their sense of self at such a young age that they have no specific memoires of being told.

Difference and belonging

The chapter on ethnicity, "race" and connectedness to different communities will look in more detail at some of the experiences of racism that these women had in childhood and as adults. The focus here is on the feelings of difference and the sense of belonging that the women experienced, or not, in their childhood.

Sixteen women (22%) said that they felt they had been treated differently in the communities where they grew up, while 47 (65%) said they had not, and nine (12.5%) said they did not know. One woman recounted an early memory of school:

I suppose the thing that kicked it off for me was when I was taken to primary and put on display in the "happy coat and trousers" that I came to England in, as a piece of show and tell. I remember being stood on a desk and having people prodding and poking at me and laughing and thinking, "why?" I think that is what started the "what is different about me?" Victoria

Some women recalled feeling at times that they did not quite belong in their families. In rare cases, like Hayley, this was felt to be quite deliberate:

I always knew I wasn't the same as my brother and sister, even though I was well fed and I was well looked after, I was never part of the family. There was always – this is so far and beyond that you can't go.

But for other women this was limited to very specific memories, usually involving their parents explaining their adoption to others and the feeling that this marked them out as different.

If we went away on holiday I can remember my mother would say, this is the family here, and they would say, 'Oh, you mean the three here' and not count me in. And my mother would say, 'No, this is my daughter as well'. They would sort of look at my mother as if to say, it can't be. And then they would look at my dad and then they would think maybe she is from his first marriage. And often, I can remember my mother introducing me to people or even to a new doctor and they would kind of look at my mother and look at me when she would say, 'This is my eldest daughter,' and then she would have to say, 'my adopted daughter'. And that would immediately make me feel well, I am not really a daughter. I don't know how she felt about it. Cathy

Peer relationships and experiences at school

From an early age, a child's interest in and the making of friendships with other children is a very important part of development. These friendships become a core part of a widening sense of the world outside the family and are the source of significant feelings of enjoyment, shared interests, identity and intimacy. Such relationships can be long lasting and their ending a source of transitory loss and pain, but for some children this can be more substantial. Relationships with other children can also be the source of tensions and conflict with bullying playing a part for some. Disappointment, upset and anxiety, and finding ways of addressing these painful feelings, can be as much a part of important learning in childhood as they are in the family experience.

Some women talked about having a small number of close friends:

I used to have a number of friends but I think there were only one or two. I didn't have masses of friends. I tended to choose one or two growing up. So I am not one of those people that have lots and lots of friends and even now, will only be a fairly small circle, and especially in my childhood I would only have one best friend. Paula

Others described themselves as quite popular:

I have always been lucky. I have always had quite a lot of friends. It is interesting that my best friend at school was also Chinese. So whether you do kind of move to like-to-like I don't know ... but she was Chinese, so growing up between the ages of 6 to 12, we had each other, and although I don't ever remember there ever being any racial problems or anything like that, I suppose we always were like best friends. Jane

A number of women spoke of feeling excluded to a greater or lesser degree. Vivian told us:

I went to an all-girls school and I didn't do boys because of being over-protected. I did not belong to one camp because I was very quiet. Sometimes they used to drop me and leave me in the corner and tease me. But I went back years ago to a reunion and they said it was just that you were very quiet ... you know. It still leaves me a bit hesitant about muscling in with people to start with. I don't want to muscle in and push in on their little crowd if I am not wanted.

She went on to add:

There were some Chinese girls but they were . . . Chinese, if you see what I mean, so I didn't sort of fit into their group and I wasn't English or Chinese to the other children so sometimes I didn't fit in their group . So I felt a bit left out. Vivian

I did have friends at school but I did have a sense of not quite fitting in and kids used to throw stones at me on my bike and call me "four-eyed chinky" and stuff like that. Molly

You know, I wasn't invited to parties. It is this thing like I wasn't included with the in-crowd. In fact, the only in-crowd that I was ever part of in primary school included the oddballs anyway, as it were . . . so the larger child, the skinny child, the ones who would not fit . . . Katy

Many of the women reported behaviour that would be seen as bullying, often perceived to be the result of their visible differences. The women responded to this in different ways; some just tried to ignore it while others dealt with it head on.

I thought to myself, well, I've got to stay at this school for a long, long time and I don't want to put up with this every day, so I asked my dad to teach me how to punch. I'm short now, I'm four foot eleven now. Anyway, the next day I took this boy behind the bike shed and I clipped him on the nose. I probably didn't hurt him because at the age of six – I think he was the year above, so he probably would have been seven – I don't think I would have really hurt him but . . . well, I know I shocked him terribly. I said to him you ever do that and push me down the stairs again and this is what I'll do to you – clonk, like that, and I was never bullied again after that. So I've always had this thing about I will not be bullied. Miranda

In terms of education, 66 (92%) of the 72 women attended state primary schools, while the others went to independent schools, faith primary schools or special stage schools; only one woman attended boarding school during childhood.

During the secondary school years, 51 women (71%) attended comprehensive schools, ten (14%) attended grammar schools, four (6%) attended faith schools and the remainder attended private fee-paying schools or independent schools. Four girls (6%) were at a boarding school for all or part of their secondary education.

Circumstances of leaving the adoptive home

All 72 women in the study had moved out of their parents' homes at an average age of just under 19 years. Fifty-two of them (62%) left home as adults at age 18 or over, nearly all before the age of 25. The most common reasons given were to start college or training, take up a job offer or look for a job, get married or move in with a partner. Only four of those who had left home as adults cited arguments, relationship difficulties or being evicted or told to leave as their main reason for leaving.

Twenty women (28%) had left home before the age of 18. Of these, five stated that they had been told to leave or had been evicted, whilst two cited arguments and one relationship difficulties as their main reason. Eleven women had left home at 16 or 17 to start training or college, take up a job offer or simply because they needed independence.

When I was 16 I left home. I think in our teens my mother found it quite difficult to understand teenagers. She was very, very good with children and had fostered many children but as soon as we reached our teens and we could, I suppose, answer back, my mother found it very difficult. I think when we all approached our teens we all left home pretty young. So I can't single myself out. So I can't put that down to being because I was adopted or because I am a different nationality. Judy

Three women described leaving their adoptive homes before adulthood due to relationship difficulties with family members that could not be resolved. One woman was placed in local authority care at age 12 following a breakdown in relationships with her adoptive parents, and two women left home at age 15 to enter into what we would now describe as a private fostering arrangement with family friends.

Conclusion

The adopted women's accounts of their experiences while growing up provide insights into the advantages, disadvantages and serious challenges that family life and adoptive family life offered these women in the UK in the 1960s. Most of the adopted women had loving homes where they felt that they were nurtured and cared for, but there were a few who had harsh family experiences where they felt unloved and unwanted. Capturing the experience of family life from the perspective of the adopted women necessitates an understanding of a wide range of factors.

For all families, security, stability, intimacy, belonging and support are complex issues that work themselves out over time to the advantage or disadvantage of the individual family members. For women with a challenging start in life – institutional care, removal and transportation to a new country and a new family with their attendant vast differences – family life has some additional significant and potentially challenging dimensions.

There is little doubt that, for the majority of these women, their recollections of their adoptive parents and their wider experiences of family and community life were largely positive. The relationships both within and outside of the adoptive families clearly play an important role in understanding the good outcomes. However, the particular pressures for those who faced what would now be recognised as a form of abuse, poor parenting or discriminatory or racist attitudes outside the home cannot be overlooked. More needs to be understood about how the experiences differ when compared with those of children adopted by parents who share their ethnic background or who were raised by their birth family. Similarly, we cannot assume the outcomes would be the same for a group of boys adopted from Hong Kong. Lastly, in exploring these issues, it is important to acknowledge the significant differences in the context of adoption during the 1960s and 70s as well as the differences in values, beliefs and attitudes about children, family life, school and community. The findings described here outline both the advantages and disadvantages experienced during childhood and adolescence that helped to shape the women's lives.

Summary

- The chapter touches on the unfamiliarity for the young child of joining an unknown and unrelated family.
- Most of the adoptive families already had children and so these adopters had prior parenting experience.
- Recollections of being parented were explored. Most of the adopted women had nurturing homes but there was a minority who reported harsh parenting where they felt unloved and unwanted
- Those women who recalled that, during childhood and adolescence, the behaviour of both parents towards them lacked warmth, understanding and acceptance, had significantly worse adult psychological adjustment.
- The context of parenting styles in this era needs to be taken into account.
- Visible difference from family and peers played an important part in childhood experience to varying degrees.
- Family relationships become more strained during adolescence.
- Relationships with siblings, peers and the wider family were largely but not entirely positive.
- The extent of open communication varied in the adoptive families. For some, their origins and adoption were freely discussed from a young age, while other women recalled being afraid or discouraged from asking questions.

6   The adult years

Introduction

One of the unique aspects of this study is that we have been able to explore what life has been like in a range of areas for the study sample, not just as children but also as adults. In the previous chapter, we reported on how the women experienced their childhood, including the relationships they developed with their adoptive families and peers. This chapter looks at the adult years.

In adulthood, family relationships are likely to undergo certain shifts and changes as roles and responsibilities change. For many women, partnerships and parenthood create new priorities; for those women who take on responsibility for caring for ageing parents, this also means a marked change in the dynamics of that relationship. Leaving the parental home and becoming independent are major markers in most people's lives. At the time when the study women began to leave the parental home, British society was undergoing rapid social change, as illustrated by the longitudinal NCDS 1958 cohort (Elliott and Vaitilingam, 2008). Women's lifestyles and standards of living began to see dramatic changes compared to those of post-war Britain and the 1950s.

One possible scenario of the long-term consequences of inadequate early nurturing would be that the sample would report high levels of difficulty across different domains of adult life. For example, this might involve a lack of significant adult relationships, multiple broken relationships, or histories of frequent poor choice in partners. This chapter explores the extent to which the women's patterns of intimate and social relationships, parenting, education and employment correspond to this picture. We also report on how the women's relationships within their adoptive families have fared over time.

Partnerships

An area of great interest was the intimate partnerships the sample had developed in their adult lives. In the questionnaire pack and during interviews, the women were asked to describe the positive and negative aspects of their relationships with their current and past partners, whether the relationship had ever broken down, and whether or not there were any specific serious problems associated with the partners they chose.

Ninety-four per cent of the women described themselves as heterosexual. Forty-six of the 72 participants (64%) were in marriages or civil partnerships at the time of completing the questionnaire pack and a further nine described themselves as cohabiting (13%). Five were separated and five divorced, making up around 14 per cent of the total, seven said they had never been married and were not in a co-habiting relationship (10%). Fifty-nine women (82%) had married or entered a civil partnership at some point; seven women (just below 10%) had been married twice. Those who described themselves as gay/lesbian were in relationships with women at the time of completing the questionnaire pack. Forty-one women (57%) were still with their first marriage or civil partner at the time of participating in the study.

Age at first marriage and length of marriage for those still married

The 59 women who had been married at least once married for the first time between the ages of 18 and 47. The youngest two married for the first time at age 18; however, 20 women married for the first time when over the age of 30, of whom six married for the first time when over the age of 40.

A number of women met their partners at a relatively young age and have been with the same person ever since. For those in a marriage or civil partnership at the time of participating in the study, eight (18%) had been in marriages or civil partnerships for 10 years or under, 19 (43%) for between 11 and 20 years, and 17 (39%) for more than 20 years. The average length of partnership at the time of participating in the study was nearly 18 years, with the longest partnership lasting 33 years and the shortest one year.

Previous marriages and significant partnerships[14]

Thiry-five participants (60% of the 59 who said they had been married or in civil partnerships at least once) stated that they had never lived with any other partners. Of the nine women who described themselves as cohabiting, almost all had lived with a different partner previously. Seven women in the study had had two marriages by the time of participating in the study; five of them were still married to their second marriage partner, whilst two were separated from the second partner.

Partners

Fifty-five of the women (76% of the total) were in relationships at the time of participating in the study and provided information about their current partner. Of these women, just over two-thirds described their partner as white British. Two described their partners as black, five as dual heritage, one as of Chinese origin and five as of European origin other than British. The remainder did not specify their partner's ethnicity.

In response to the question: 'Thinking about your former partners, have they tended to share the same ethnicity as you?' 59 participants (82%) stated that they had never had a Chinese partner.

In general, most spoke positively about their current partners/ husbands with some acknowledgement that long-term marriages and partnerships could prove challenging at times:

Just nice being with someone who is a friend and a partner. I like being married. It has its difficulties but generally I think that is what I have always wanted, to be married to someone. [He's] a good dad and very practical in terms of not DIY but doing things

---

14 Percentages in this sub-section are calculated out of the 59 women who have been married or entered a civil partnership at least once unless stated otherwise.

for us as a family. He is organised with admin and stuff. I still fancy him. Isobel

Well, you know, he is solid. We have a laugh. And he is like a soulmate really. I mean we went through a rough patch and that was through his mother coming between us and this was when we were married. Florence

He is just such a stable individual, you know, he is . . . what can I say? He is the rock in my life I suppose. Rosemary

By contrast, there were examples in the interviews – as you would expect in a sample of women in their 40s and 50s – of relationship breakdowns or instability linked to infidelity or incompatibility. External stresses, such as job losses or tense relationships with in-laws, had put some partnerships under strain. Although these experiences were reported as distressing, there did not appear to be consistent evidence for widespread patterns of psychological difficulties in forming and maintaining close bonds.

Parenting

Fifty-one (71%) of the 72 participants had given birth to or had adopted at least one child by the time of participating in the study. The maximum number of children was five (two participants) and the average number of children for all women (including those without children) was 1.5. For the 51 participants who were parents, the average number of children was 2.1. The average age at which partici-pants became parents for the first time was 30.5 years, with the youngest mother aged 20 and the oldest 42.

Among the UK-born women who participated in the 1958 National Child Development Study, two-thirds of them had at least one child by the age of 30 (Elliot and Vaitilingam, 2008, p 21) and by the age of 40, this figure had risen to 82 per cent. Although this proportion is higher than the study sample who became mothers (71%), this difference should be interpreted with caution given the range of factors that may influence child-bearing. Alongside individual

Table 6.1
Number of children for each participant

No children	29% (n = 21)
1 child	14% (n = 10)
2 children	42% (n = 30)
3 children	11% (n = 8)
4 or more children	4% (n = 3)

differences in motivation and choice around parenthood, two other factors may be relevant. First, the average age for first-time motherhood among the NCDS women rose with the level of education. As will be reported later in this chapter, the study women were educationally well-qualified. Second, rates of childbirth have decreased for women in the UK over time and the slightly later average year of birth for the sample may have played a role.

Altogether four women in our study had adopted children, all girls; three of those adopted from China or Hong Kong. Two of these women have adopted one girl each and the other two have adopted two girls. In contrast to many of the adoptive families this group of women grew up in, only one of the women has birth children as well as adopted children. On average, the women were 37 years old when they adopted for the first time.

During the interviews we asked the women about the positive aspects of parenting and how they dealt with any challenges that arose. The vast majority described parenting as a positive experience with comments such as: 'Best thing I have ever done' (Audrey); 'My greatest achievement'; 'Took to it like a duck to water – it was great' (Emily). For the most part, they took pride in their children's behaviour and attitudes. There had been no sustained social services involvement regarding child protection concerns, with one exception. Common stresses in raising children, particularly young babies and adolescents, were accepted as part and parcel of parenting:

She can be a pain in the arse but that's her job as a teenager.
Victoria

Whilst a few women in the study explained that they had made a conscious decision not to become mothers, others told us that they were curious about having their own children as it meant that they would meet a blood relative for the first time in their lives. When Jennifer became pregnant, she and her husband were doubly curious as they had both been adopted:

It was wonderful. Because we are both adopted it was our own flesh and blood. People kept saying, Oh, I wonder if it will come out more Chinese or more English, more white . . . ? With blue eyes or black eyes? Or will it come out ginger? There were quite a few comments about that from both sides of the family.
Jennifer

Friendships

As well as asking about family relationships, we wanted to find out how the women viewed their friendships with others outside the family. Patterns of friendship were mixed: some described having a large circle of friends from different periods of life and others preferred to maintain a smaller number of long-term friendships. Such confiding relationships were highly valued. Within these descriptions, a number of the women reported feeling reticent in opening up to new people, and many described themselves as private or reserved.

There is always still a bit of . . . less so now . . . of guardedness. I'm sure my friendships could be more fulfilling if I was able to just completely let go, but I am not willing to do that just yet.
Molly

The idea of preferring to have a small number of close friends, or sometimes even just one, came across strongly:

I have about three or four – I'm not one for having lots of close friends, not my thing really . . . I am actually quite cautious of meeting new people. Penny

I am not one for having loads of friends who are not true friends. I would prefer to have the one true friend. And my mum of course. Alison

Of course these feelings were not universal and some of the women described themselves as very sociable:

Oh god, I've got loads – I've got a lot of friends, but I would say six very close friends, so that's nice. Eva

Eighteen participants specifically mentioned having Chinese friends and various participants mentioned having friends of other nationalities and backgrounds, as Belinda recounted:

When I went to university, I lived with a girl who spoke Welsh, another friend was from Guyana so she was black, and me and another girl who I haven't kept in touch with so much. I can remember walking into the pub with my flatmates and the person in the bar said, 'Is this the UN that's just walked in?' (laughs) Because we were all of a different colour. Belinda

However, to an extent this was determined by the place in which they settled. Other participants described very different experiences:

I have never had a Chinese friend, I am not saying that if I had met someone Chinese and they wanted to be my friend and I would say, oh no, I just haven't met anyone Chinese. Hayley

Confiding relationships

In asking the women about their partnerships and friendships, we wanted to know whether they had someone they could turn to for support or other help in their personal life, and whether they could talk frankly and share their feelings with him or her. The women nearly all (97%) reported having a confidante to whom they could turn for such support. This group included some women who described very strained (or non-existent) relationships with adoptive family members in adulthood, as discussed later in this chapter. A similar proportion of both the adopted and non-adopted comparison groups from NCDS reported being able to confide in someone.

One theme that emerged from the interview data was the high proportion of women who gave examples of being "proud to be independent" or described themselves as either self-contained or self-reliant. These were spontaneous descriptions of their beliefs and perspectives about themselves rather than a response to a specific question we asked. A few women wondered whether their attitudes were in some way shaped by their early experiences. Independence was seen by some as a positive attribute that helped them to cope with life's challenges. Others suggested that it sometimes meant they kept others at a distance or felt distrustful. Without comparative data we are unable to say whether this was a specific characteristic of this group. We have considered the possibility that some developed a protective "steeling" effect in response to their experiences of early adversity (Rutter, 2012).

Educational attainment across the lifetime

In reviewing the information collected for this section, the picture that emerges is of a highly educated group of women. Nearly all participants agreed that educational attainment had been important to them and left school with some qualifications.

Forty-two per cent achieved A levels, AS levels or Scottish Highers. Some gained vocational qualifications after leaving school in areas including secretarial, catering and nursing training. More than a third of the women went to university (26 women gained a Bachelor's degree at a higher education institute). By contrast, 11 per cent of women who participated in the 1958 NCDS had completed a degree by age 33 (Elliot and Vaitilingam, 2008, p 9). Thirteen of the women in our study gained an additional qualification such as a Master's degree or post-graduate certificate or diploma, and one participant had completed a PhD. An additional 15 women achieved a Higher National Diploma (HND) or Higher National Certificate (HNC). A number of women returned to education later in life. One woman was in full-time education at the time of filling in the questionnaire pack, whilst six others had completed an educational qualification between the ages of 25 and 40.

Figure 6.1
Highest qualification to date as specified by participants[15]

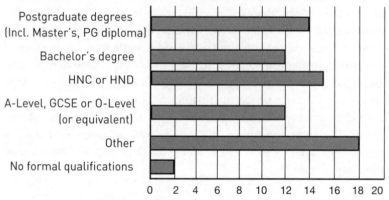

Of the 18 women who listed qualifications categorised as "other", six referred to membership of a professional body or exams that would usually require a Bachelor's degree. The remainder included nursing, midwifery or paramedic registration and incomplete Bachelor's degrees.

15 In grouping these qualifications, we used a compressed version of the Framework for Higher Education Qualifications (FHEQ) and the National Qualifications Framework (NQF). Full details of the classifications used in these frameworks can be accessed at: http://webarchive.nationalarchives.gov.uk/20121015000000/ www.direct.gov.uk/en/EducationAndLearning/QualificationsExplained/ DG_10039017 (accessed 12 Dec 2012).

Career and employment

At the time of participating in the study, 54 (75%) of the 72 women were in some type of employment, 34 full time and 20 part time. Of those who were not in work, one was seeking employment, five (7%) were permanently or temporarily unable to work for health reasons, 11 (15%) said they were looking after the home or family and one was retired.

The information from the study shows us that the women went into wide-ranging careers and employment and like many other women of their generation, some decided to change career or gain other qualifications during their adult years.

Fifty-three women specified the field of work in which they were currently working or their most recent employment. Eighteen women (34%) entered the nursing and social care field, including alternative therapies (two participants); 11 (21%) were in managerial and professional jobs; seven (13%) were in the teaching profession; five (9%) were in administration and clerical jobs; four (8%) were in the creative arts and media, including new media; four (8%) were in service industries (for example, catering or retail); two were in the legal profession; and two were in finance.

Nineteen women did not specify their current or previous main job, usually because they were not employed at the time.

Support from adoptive parents in adulthood

We know from the previous chapter that most – but not all – described relatively good relationships within their adoptive family during childhood and we were interested in whether this had continued or changed in later life. We have reported earlier that the women's recollections of their parents' behaviour towards them in childhood and adolescence predicted their current psychological adjustment. This section explores in more detail the women's relationships with their adoptive parents. How did these relationships change over time, particularly as they established adult lives and perhaps got married, had children or developed careers? What did the women pick out as being particularly positive or negative aspects? Did they feel that being adopted marked these relationships in some way?

Given that a particular strength of this study was the lifespan perspective, we wanted to explore in some depth relationships with adoptive parents from the adopted person's point of view. We summarise here the women's reports looking back over the years on how they have come to relate to and view their parents in adulthood. Some of these features were naturally similar to what might be expected of any adult, adopted or not, describing relationships with their parents. Others described ways in which being adopted had in their view affected the way they and/or their parents relate to and communicate with each other.

All of the women at the time they participated in this study were living independently from their adoptive parents. However, the majority reported that their adoptive parents had offered some form of support after the point at which they left home. This included financial support (46%); help with accommodation (31%); childcare (13%); some listed emotional support or paying for one-off events such as a wedding. Although there was a small group who had little contact with their adoptive parents as adults, in most cases adoptive family members were seen as a valuable source of support.

> *Well, I've had a really good life, money was no object and my mother and father gave me a good education and if you look back, what would I have had in Hong Kong? They have been very, very good to me and certainly obviously now in later life, with my daughter and my son and everything, they are very helpful.*
> Barbara

Josephine was also very appreciative of the help and support her parents were able to give her, particularly following the breakdown of her marriage and the birth of her child.

> *Because I had my parents, when things went bad, I immediately had a secure safe place to go and as soon as I was with my parents, I did not have a financial burden. I wasn't going to*

starve so there was never a point where I felt 'how am I going to feed us?' So I was very lucky in that respect.

Relationships with adoptive parents and changes over time

At the time of the study, 56 women reported that their adoptive mothers were still alive and 31 had adoptive fathers still alive. For most of those who had lost a parent, this had occurred during adulthood, on average in their mid-thirties. Nine women had lost a parent before turning 18. Four sets of adoptive parents divorced during the participant's adulthood, and one set separated. In the study we looked specifically at how the relationship with the adoptive parents altered over time, particularly in how close the women felt to their parents.

Figure 6.2 shows that 63 per cent said that they got along with their adoptive mothers most of the time as opposed to 73 per cent in childhood and 49 per cent in adolescence. We were interested in whether there was a correspondence between women's current feelings and their recollections of their childhood. We found there was no significant change (McNemar's test). Most women responded similarly for both childhood and adulthood. However, 13 per cent indicated that the relationships were worse in adulthood while six per cent reported an improvement.

In terms of their relationships with their adoptive fathers, the numbers of women who said they got along well most of the time are slightly higher for each stage of life so far. Here, 82 per cent said that they got along most of the time in childhood, 65 per cent in adolescence and 69 per cent in adulthood. Again, we found there was no significant change over time. Most women (85%) got along with their adoptive fathers when young and as adults, while nine per cent did not get along at either time. Six per cent of women had got along with their adoptive father during childhood but not in later life.

Figure 6.2
How well did you get along with your adoptive mother?[16]

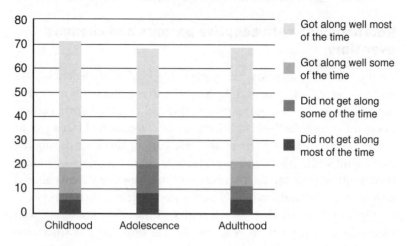

Figure 6.3
How well did you get along with your adoptive father?[17]

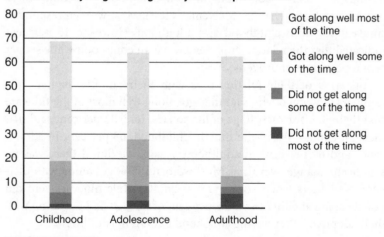

16 Childhood n = 72; adolescence n = 69; adulthood n = 69. Most missing data relate to deceased adoptive parents.

17 Childhood n = 69; adolescence n = 65; adulthood n = 64. Missing data mostly relate to deceased adoptive parents.

We were interested in whether those women who recalled a lack of acceptance and/or warmth from their adoptive parents during childhood also described greater difficulties in getting on with them in adulthood. We checked the responses for those women who recalled their adoptive parents' care favourably and found very few cases in which they reported not getting on well with their adoptive parents in adulthood. We found, however, that of the 14 women reporting "low care" from both parents (see Chapter 4, p 62), nearly half of the group reported getting along relatively well with their adoptive parents in adulthood, as shown below. This was true of both mothers and fathers, although slightly more so for fathers. Therefore, a reported experience of poor care during childhood did not necessarily predict poor relationships with adoptive parents in adulthood.

Table 6.2
Relationship with adoptive mother

	Gets along well with adoptive mother in adulthood	Does not get along well with adoptive mother in adulthood
"Low care" from adoptive mother during childhood (n = 21)	9	12

Table 6.3
Relationship with adoptive father

	Gets along well with adoptive father in adulthood	Does not get along well with adoptive father in adulthood
"Low care" from adoptive father during childhood (n = 16)	8	8

As well as asking about how well they got on, we also asked about how close the women would describe these relationships as being. Where the adoptive parents were still alive, 72 per cent said that they felt very close or quite close to their adoptive mothers in adulthood compared to 67 per cent for adoptive fathers. For those whose parents were deceased, 80 per cent said that they had been close to their adoptive mother when she was alive and 63 per cent had been close to their father.

Figure 6.4
Current/most recent relationship with adoptive parents

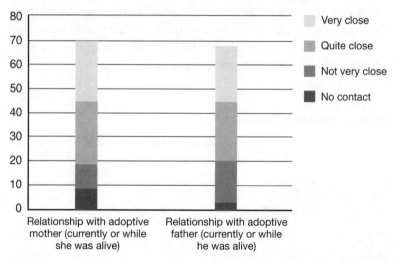

During the interviews we explored further the details of these relationships and what the women meant by feeling close or not to their adoptive parents. Some told us that they had retained very close relationships from childhood and described supportive and loving relationships that had not changed over time. Others reported that the relationship improved, deteriorated or had shifted in some way. The following quotes illustrate some of the different types of relationships described.

Closeness to adoptive parent(s) – No change

Some participants described that they had always felt close to their adoptive parent(s) and this had not altered over time. Some felt that their parent was "in tune" with their moods and that they could turn to them for advice and comfort.

I was thinking, out of the whole of my life if someone says to me who are the most important people in my life, they'd be my granddad, my mum and dad, and my two children . . . and the dog! Maxine

It is funny really, because Mum knows when I am down and I think you do if you have your own children . . . you know when they are down. Mum always says when I ring up, she says, I know your voice, something is not right here. Florence

Some of the women also described how the warmth and love they received from their parents was also very much felt by the next generation – the women's own children – as Josephine recounts:

They all adore my dad . . . They go in [to his house], you know, they kick their shoes off, they flop about his house and out come the toys. Daddy puts CBeebies on. Josephine

For Erica, participating in the study made her review her relationship with her adoptive mother, who was still alive and to whom she felt very close. She also reported what happened when she told her mother about participating in the study:

This study has prompted really nice conversations with Mum. I feel quite privileged to be able to hear her side of it really. It's very nice, it's very special. I think she likes it. It's not that she's had an empty life, she's had a very full life but she's quite pleased to be asked. She's certainly been very generous with information about things. Erica

Jackie explained how her relationship with her mother never really changed and that she felt she was still the child. She explained that she would have liked to have had more open discussion. She did not describe their lack of closeness as due to the adoption, but just the way her mother was and, in her view, typical of that generation.

As a child it was fine, and in adolescence – but when it came to being an adult, I did find my mum was very much the mother and I was the daughter. I never felt we could be on the same par really. It wasn't as open as I would have liked. Mum wouldn't ask questions so I always felt like it was me that had to open up first, before I'd get any sort of response . . . But again, that's her upbringing, it's her generation. They very much sort of kept their emotions together and didn't express them in the way that perhaps people do now. Jackie

Angela felt that her parents never really understood her and although she says that they did the best for her she does not feel that they get on as adults. She wonders if this was because she was too compliant as a child and did not make her voice and views known to them.

I didn't have massive arguments with them as an adolescent, which you'd expect. I think probably, looking back, it might have been better if I had rebelled and made a stamp of who I really was, rather than trying to please and sort of do things the way that they want. I don't get on with my parents, they were absolutely motivated by the best of intentions and they tried their best in their way, I do think they did do that. Angela

Shifts in relationships to adoptive parent(s) in adulthood

As reported in the preceding chapter, parenting styles have changed over time and some of the women recalled their family life as being quite formal and distant in some ways during childhood. Faith explained that in her case this changed when she became an adult.

It was quite a formal kind of family. You did not ask questions, for example, you did not say anything at the dinner table unless

you were spoken to. Certainly my mother, who was really in charge of the family, treated me in a very particular kind of a way when I was under-age and as soon as I turned 18 she treated me like I was an adult, which really took me by surprise... The first time I went back home after being at university, during the first term, Mum was a friend.

Valerie told us that how she became closer at the time when her adoptive mother became ill. She said that up until that time her mother's lack of warmth had permeated through her childhood and adolescence and continued into adulthood.

But then she became so ill, we were able to get closer to her, which was the first time for all us kids. Perhaps she had to because she had no one else. Dad had died. It was funny though, because once I said to her, 'I do love you, Mum,' and she said, 'Oh, thank you very much,' as if I was admiring her hat, but she didn't say 'I love you'.

Some shift in the relationship but still not close
In childhood and adolescence, Cathy had a very difficult and fraught relationship with her mother, who was very strict and did not show affection. Cathy considers that whilst the relationship has improved to some extent, the shadow of the past lingers on.

My mother gets very controlling. I think my father would be a warmer person but my mother won't allow it. My mother is cold, very cold, and when you have lived with somebody for so long like that, you end up just having to conform. I think my mother now wishes she was a lot warmer but it is too late.

Belonging to a family
Ruth told us that she feels very much part of a family and that she was loved by her parents when they were alive, but made comparisons with other families.

I don't think we're as close as some families that I observe. My family's quite reserved, quite English, quite unemotional but I don't think we're not close in a sense that I can always pick up the phone . . . and we get on very well, we hardly ever argue, you know, we have no issues. Ruth

Nina thought that her family wished she would confide in them more and that she perhaps had a different approach to dealing with her feelings compared with her siblings. They had always maintained contact and there had been times when conversations opened up.

My mum was only saying to me a few weeks ago, that 'you have got this chip on your shoulder about being the black sheep of the family. You are not,' she goes, 'if anybody is more loved in this family then it is you because I didn't pick the rest of them but I picked you,' which I thought was a really nice thing to say, you know, considering that we don't really talk at that level. It was quite a nice thing for her to say. Nina

Reflections on nature and nurture

Adopted people, like twins, have been the subject of empirical studies that examine how genetic traits, environmental influences and inter-actions between the two contribute to an individual's characteristics, such as personality and behaviour. It was interesting that some of the participants in this study also gave some thought to this and considered that no matter how much love or support their parents gave them, it would not alter who they were and the genetic inheritance they were born with.

Helen stated that the way she feels towards her adoptive mother and family is to do with her genetic make-up. She told us that she is naturally more remote than her siblings and other family members.

I feel sorry for my mum in so much as I'm not naturally a very "close" kind of person, it's just not the kind of person I am. My sister was different to me, she was kind of more childlike

anyway, but I kind of think we're fairly close but I wouldn't say we're really, really close. I mean, I ring them all the time but I don't think we're really close . . . and that's just me. I think I would be always like that. It's just who I am and I've realised it's not because I'm adopted, it's not because of my mum. It's just who I am.

In contrast, Gill described how she in fact felt very similar in personality to her adoptive mother.

It is funny because in some ways I probably got on better with my mother than my sister, who is her birth child. It is not because my mother did not love us any more or less than the other, but my mother and I had very similar interests. She was very girly. She loved dollies and she liked clothes. She liked going out shopping whereas my older sister hates shopping, is not interested in clothes.

In Brenda's family, the idea of what makes a person who they are was explicitly discussed.

The whole family talks about nature and nurture. As far as nurture is concerned, I think that we are all very similar in that we are caring and we are a close family and we care about each other and how we are doing and so on . . . [In terms of nature] the way they put it was that I am very lucky because I have not got the neuroticism and that side of it. There is a certain amount of obsessive behaviour and nerves and I haven't got that, so yes, I am lucky in that sense. So yes, I am glad I am adopted.

Gail and her family also talked about family dynamics and when asked about the gains and losses of adoption, she reflected:

Well, obviously having this family, you know, my mum and dad and siblings and a very secure, happy childhood . . . I suppose the only negative thing, coming into a family, maybe, is having a very different personality. But they might see it as positive because I'm always the social person, bringing the family together.

Joan told us about a recent experience that she considered really significant at a reunion of extended family members.

I remember on the family tree chart I was a dotted line rather than a solid line and I remember thinking, 'Oh, you know, but I am . . . why aren't I a solid line? I wish I was a solid line.' That was quite funny actually. But it wasn't . . . it was kind of like jokey, but I did notice it. Everybody was a solid line and I was, like, you know . . .

Maintaining contact with the adoptive parents and the adoptive family

Just over a third of those women whose adoptive mothers were still alive reported visiting more than once a month and a third of this group more than once a week. About half visit less than once a month but reasons for this included geographical distance. Eight of the women said they have no contact with their adoptive mother at all. Although fewer adoptive fathers were still alive (31 in comparison to 56 mothers), the proportions of reported contact are remarkably similar.

As for the previous question, the interviews allowed the women to describe in more detail how family contact operated and the feelings associated with this. For Belinda, family get-togethers were a regular feature of adult life.

. . . and my mother's thing, her whole life is to keep the family together – we always take holidays together, regardless of who is doing what.

For some of the women, the contact was limited because of other family commitments or the distance they lived from their adoptive

Figure 6.5
Contact with adoptive parents

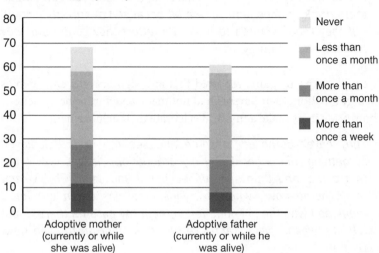

parents' home. Maria was among those who reported less regular contact but this was due to the practicalities of finding opportunities to all meet up.

> *Oh, when we do eventually all get together, which isn't very often, we have a brilliant time. It is really good. It was Mum's birthday about a month ago and we all, most us, got out to Mum and Dad's. Not all the grandchildren but all the daughters went out there and it was brilliant.*

Some participants said that, although they did keep in contact with their adoptive family, they felt that they were the ones who had to make the effort. Lesley told us that her parents never came to visit her even though it was not out of their way when visiting other family members.

> *I say to them you can always pop in here be it on the way round or on the way back and their argument is, well, it's a bit out of*

the way, and I'm thinking it's not that much off the motorway, but as they say you can take a horse to water but you can't make them drink. It does annoy me a bit because I'm sure they could – if they really wanted to make the effort they could, but they haven't, so . . . Lesley

A couple of participants reported that at a significant event, such as their graduation, their parents had not made an effort to be present or show pride in or make a fuss and celebrate their achievement.

They never bothered to come and see me or if I achieved something, like when I had my graduation, it was only Mum that came, and then she rushed home and said, 'Oh, I've got to go home now', when everyone else was taken out for a meal, so I was the only one left without my parents there. I just felt she wasn't proud, and I've had that right up to even now. Diane

Angela told us that she continues to keep in contact with her adoptive family but finds the relationship with her adoptive mother difficult, which harks back to childhood experiences.

There are quite a lot of memories of things that are quite unpleasant that are very hurtful – it goes very, very deep as you can probably feel . . . So, on the whole, I just don't think about it and I don't particularly like to have that much to do with her because that way I don't need to think about it basically. So I don't even like to hear her voice on the phone actually.

For the eight women no longer in contact with their adoptive parent(s), there was a range of reasons as to why this happened. The youngest was 16 years old when she left home and made a decision to stop contact with all members of her adoptive family, due to ongoing difficulties in these relationships.

Another woman, Jade, recounted that, when she was growing up, her mother would give her the silent treatment and not talk to her for weeks as a form of punishment. Over the years Jade decided that this was not acceptable. She described this childhood experience of being "sent to Coventry" as having had an impact on her later life.

The last, ten – twelve years, it's changed. I just guess I'd got to an age where I think I don't need to put up with this behaviour from her any more. She would go weeks without talking to whoever was out of favour, so you know she wouldn't speak to you for two weeks, which is horrendous I think. I'd never do that. With my husband now, if we ever have words or have a row, he can then do this non-speaking and I say to him, 'You can't do that, I can't deal with that'.

But in Emily's case it was her mother who refused to have contact. She too described her childhood and adolescent relationship with her mother as an unhappy one.

She'd barred my number – what a bitch, you know? So what's the point of adopting? Why did she ever, ever, ever adopt me?

For Jocelyn, her adoptive mother not only rejected contact but also banned her from seeing her siblings, although they kept in touch secretly.

Relationships with siblings over time

Participants were also asked to rate how they got on with their siblings during different periods of their life. As Figure 6.6 shows, relationships were generally positive. Thirteen participants reported that they did not get along some or most of the time with their siblings during adolescence, but by adulthood this had reduced to eight women. Two participants grew up as only children and a further five participants not included in Figure 6.6 reported that the variance in their relationships with individual siblings made the question difficult to answer.

As with any family, there was a wide range of different styles of sibling relationships and for some women these relationships were

Figure 6.6
How well did/do you get on with your siblings?*

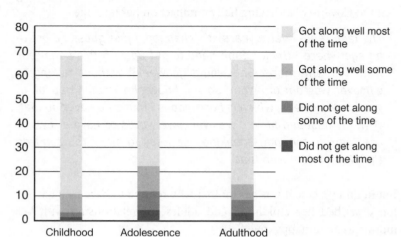

highly valued. When asked to whom they would turn for advice and emotional support, nine participants said it would be a sibling.

Brenda, who grew up with several siblings and was also close to her adoptive mother, told us:

They are my closest friends. They really are because I don't have any really close friends. That does sound sad, doesn't it? I think my family are my closest friends. I really do.

As with their adoptive parents, the majority of participants were in touch with siblings to varying degrees but, in a few cases, contact had ceased altogether. Again, several participants mentioned living at considerable geographic distance from siblings; for some this meant regular telephone contact and visits when possible while for others such contact was minimal.

Reduced closeness in relationships with siblings was sometimes seen as a natural consequence of adult life with partners, children and other responsibilities taking priority. This was not always a source of distress nor seen as a consequence of adoption:

None of us keep in contact with each other much at all. I mean there are families without adopted children who are just cut off from siblings. I certainly don't ring my brothers. I don't ring my sisters that much either, but when I do, we get on alright. Lesley

Others made conscious decisions to limit their contact with a particular brother or sister if the relationship had proved problematic:

[My] brother bullied me as a child, still does if he gets a chance, hence we have little adult contact. He bullies my sister too, so I believe adoption [is] not a cause but something he could use to get at me. Faith

Conclusion

Based on the traditional social indicators covered in this chapter, what emerges is a mainly positive picture of these women's lives. Educational progress had been important to the majority and this was generally reflected in subsequent employment histories. Although some had experienced difficulties in these areas, this was not at the level of chronic problems. Relationships with adoptive family members, partners and children, for the most part, showed little evidence of atypical or extreme patterns across the group, with some notable exceptions. Most were currently in partnerships and many reported long-term stable living arrangements. In some cases, fraught or distant childhood relationships with adoptive parents had continued into later life stages but others had established better relationships after leaving home. In later chapters, we examine in more detail aspects of these women's lives that are specifically linked to their experiences of being internationally and mainly transracially adopted.

Summary

- The majority of the sample were currently married or in partnerships; average length of relationship/marriage to date was nearly 18 years. Most partners were white British.
- Two-thirds of the women have children; the average number being two.
- Nearly all left school with some qualifications; more than a third have Bachelor's and/or post-graduate degrees.
- Three-quarters of the women were employed. A third were working or had worked in nursing or social care-related fields.
- The majority got along some/most of the time with both adoptive parents across the lifespan. Where relationships had been difficult in childhood or adolescence, these had improved for half of those women by adulthood. Many had enjoyed continuing supportive relationships in their adult years.
- Around one in ten had ceased contact with their adoptive parent(s) and the context for this was often distressing.
- The majority were in touch with their siblings and got on well most of the time.

7 Health and well-being

Introduction and background

In recent years researchers have started to identify some of the health and well-being difficulties that may affect children who have spent time in institutional care (Rutter and the ERA team 1998; Vorria *et al*, 2003; Miller, 2005). In addition, certain health conditions are known to be more prevalent in particular regions of the world and there are also epidemiological, cultural and ethnic factors which may contribute to physical health outcomes.

The details of the orphanage experience have already been described in Chapter 4 but given their special relevance to health questions, a quick reminder may be helpful. The children arrived at the four main orphanages at various ages. Some were as young as a few weeks, with the eldest being three years old. Over half (53%) of our study participants entered the orphanages within a month of their estimated birth date, 32 per cent between one and six months of age and 15 per cent over six months of age. The girls spent, on average, 20 months in orphanage care before being placed with families in the UK for adoption (range 8–72 months). When we checked for bias, we found no evidence for significant differences on baseline variables, except that non-participants (from the original group of 100 girls) had a slightly later age at entry into orphanage care.

The records held at ISS UK about these adoptions included a report for each child on a medical examination undertaken a few days prior to their leaving the orphanage. Each report was signed and the names indicated that a small group of local doctors carried out the examinations, with one doctor completing 59 per cent of these reports.

The examinations included height and weight measurements, blood test results and a record of the child's immunisation. Although generally consistent, not all reports were completed fully, which makes it difficult to calculate Body Mass Index or other measurements based on this information. The medical practitioner also recorded a subjective view of whether or not the child was malnourished. Physical examinations identified any past or ongoing health problems. This included any recorded disabilities such as cleft palate, cleft lip, squint or polio. Some of these conditions had been corrected by surgery and some not.

The files also contained descriptions of the orphanages and we were therefore able to build up a picture of the environments in which the children grew up. The children were fed mainly rice porridge (congee) which sometimes included vegetables and meat. Based on these reports, their diet does not appear to have included adequate amounts of vegetables, fruits, meat or fish. This would have resulted in a lack of protein and vitamins in particular. The children also had varying amounts of milk, biscuits, juice and water. Over half (55%) of the children were noted to be slightly or moderately malnourished at examination.

Many children had low haemoglobin levels and iron deficiency anaemia, which is a reflection of a poor diet. A third of the children (30%) were described as slightly or moderately clinically anaemic. Several had high white cell counts signifying onging or underlying infection with accompanying descriptions of various minor ailments, such as colds. It is not clear whether these problems were a consequence of orphanage care or pre-dated their admission.

We noted earlier that the four main orphanages where the girls lived ranged in size from accommodating between 65 and 450 children, with a staff to child ratio ranging from 1:6 to 1:22. In those orphanages with fewer resources, children were often left to feed themselves or two children were fed from the same bowl; hence the normal coaxing a parent may do to encourage a child to eat would not have been possible. In one orphanage it was reported that the children had little room to crawl and clearly this would have had an impact on general development.

A child's growth and development are intrinsically linked. The presence of a safe and consistent primary carer may influence developmental progress in all areas: gross-motor, fine-motor, eye-hand coordination, speech and language, social skills, cognitive skills, and the development of secure attachment. We can guess that, particularly in the case of the less well-resourced orphanages, it would have been less likely for these children to have had one primary carer with sufficient time and the emotional investment necessary to promote optimum development.

The medical reports included details about the child's development and the majority were described as "normal" (73%). The following are examples of descriptions from two children's reports by ISS Hong Kong caseworkers that were sent to ISS UK:

At 12 months she was staggering about the cot while holding onto the railing, making baby-talk.

At seven months, [she] sits firmly without support, responds alertly to sounds, follows moving objects with her eyes, grasps pen or finger, neck erect.

In some cases the comments illustrate that the children's development was delayed (27%):

At 5–6 months she rolled over; 8–9 months sat without support; at 24 months stand without support; at 28 months learning to walk.

As the level of details in these reports varied and a number of different caseworkers were involved, it was not possible to develop an index of each individual child's development. However, the picture that emerges is more positive than that of children from severely depriving institutions such as those in Romania (Rutter *et al*, 1998) or where it is known that birth parents were at high risk for learning disabilities (Vorria *et al*, 2006).

With this information from the records in mind, one of the areas we wanted to explore at follow-up was whether or not our participants had developed health problems related to their early orphanage care. Are their health outcomes better than children who were not placed for adoption? Although we did not have access to data on those children who remained in the orphanages, using data available from the NCDS we explored how the study women compared at adult follow-up with matched groups of women in the UK on selected physical health outcomes.

Recollections of being told about health problems

Seven of the women who participated in the study had what were then recorded as "disabilities", such as those recorded on the ISS UK files. Two women told us that they thought that when they were matched with their adoptive parents in the UK, the fact that they had a health problem was taken into account.

> My adoptive father was a doctor. He chose to adopt me as he knew what operations I needed (for a squint) and how to arrange them.

> I had polio . . . a weakness in my lower leg. My parents chose to adopt me because I had that.

One went on to explain that, as she grew up, 'having a disability was a bigger issue than being Chinese'. Another reported:

> I was told [that when] I was a baby I was pretty sickly . . . and developmentally pretty delayed – couldn't sit up, wasn't having any solid food. That's probably why I was adopted so young . . . that's probably what saved my life really . . . I probably stood a much better chance here. Erica

As will be described in the next chapter, prejudice was a recurring feature for many after arriving in the UK and sadly this extended in some cases to the health profession. As Maureen recalls:

> I used to get recurrent bronchitis and apparently when I arrived . . . my mum had to take me straight to the doctors and he was quite . . . prejudiced . . . and he said the climate doesn't suit her and she should go back to her country . . . my mum had to stand there and fight.

Health in adulthood

When exploring the health of our participants into adulthood, we wondered how their early experiences, including lack of varied and nutritious diet and restricted opportunities to explore their environments, may have impacted on their general health.

We are aware that adequate antenatal nutrition (health and diet in pregnancy) is extremely important for the growth and development of the baby whilst in the womb and for a healthy outcome at delivery. Babies born early and/or underweight have increased difficulties and infant mortality rates. We now know that poor nutrition in pregnancy may also lead to health problems in the offspring in later life.

Professor David Barker identified that low birthweight is associated with an increased risk of hypertension, coronary heart disease, stroke and Type 2 diabetes. This is known as the Barker hypothesis (Barker, 1995). Moreover, he identified that the risk of later chronic disease is further increased if a baby has low weight gain after birth so that at two years the child is thin or stunted. After the age of two, rapid weight gain further increases the risk of later coronary heart disease, hypertension, and Type 2 diabetes (Barker *et al*, 2002). However, it has been shown that the risk of coronary heart disease was not elevated among women with lower birth weight who remained relatively lean in adult life (Rich-Edwards *et al*, 2004).

As noted earlier, data about the birth parents are not available as in most cases no information was recorded on the files. Given the situation in Hong Kong at the time (described in Chapter 1), it seems possible that some of the children may have suffered adversity in the womb as birth mothers were unlikely to have had good antenatal care and adequate dietary intake in pregnancy. It is possible, although not known for certain, that some may have had low birthweights.

We therefore asked the 72 participants specifically about heart disease, diabetes and hypertension. None of the women disclosed heart problems. No participants had diabetes (although one (1%) had developed gestational diabetes – in pregnancy only). Diabetes was present in one per cent of the NCDS cohort. Six participants (9%)

disclosed hypertension with four (6%) being on treatment. In the NCDS cohort, 12 per cent had hypertension with six per cent having required treatment in the preceding 12 months.

It is interesting to note that initial information volunteered by the participants in the study does not show increased problems in these areas. We do not have sufficient information available to look at individual growth patterns for the women. As they are currently in their 40s and 50s, it is also difficult to make comparisons as they are younger than other cohorts that have been studied in relation to these issues (for example, the Hertfordshire birth cohort born between 1923–1930 (Syddall *et al*, 2005a and 2005b); the Helskinki birth cohort born between 1924–1944 (Barker *et al*, 2009) or the Dutch famine birth cohort born between 1944–1945 (Painter *et al*, 2005)).

It is possible that such problems may increase as the women grow older and therefore a more longitudinal review would help to explore this. Good nutrition and a healthy lifestyle following adoption and indeed into adulthood may have significantly modified the increased risk of these chronic health conditions.

Height and weight
The heights of our participants ranged from 4 feet 8 inches to 5 feet 6 inches with an average height of 5 feet 2 inches (157.5cm). Whilst we do not have a direct comparison for other children born in Hong Kong at the time, we are able to look at average heights of adult (18 year old) Chinese women from data collected in 1965. Their average height was 5 feet 1 inch (155.6 cms) and data collected in 2005 showed an average height of 5 feet 3 inches (160 cms) (Li *et al*, 2009). The study participants therefore have comparable heights. Research into the effects of the Chinese famine has shown a reduction in height in women born in 1958 and 1959 in rural areas in certain parts of China. This is not directly comparable, but provides interesting evidence of dietary deprivation around birth and its effect on height attainment (Huang *et al*, 2010).

The self-reported weights of our participants ranged from 41 to 68 kilos, with an average weight of 54 kilos (8 stone 7lbs), which is broadly comparable with weight data on Chinese adults collated in 2005 (range 40–68 kg with 50th centile – 50 kg) (Li et al, 2009).

One-third of our sample (33%) considered themselves to be slightly overweight with seven per cent considering themselves to be very overweight. Over half (55%) considered their weight was about right. The NCDS data show that, by comparison, 45 per cent of age-matched women in the UK felt they were slightly overweight with 19 per cent being very overweight and only 32 per cent feeling their weight was about right.

Health and disability

Our study showed that 85 per cent of participants described their health as good or excellent compared with other people of their own age. This was very similar to the NCDS groups: 84 per cent of NCDS adopted women and 82 per cent in the non-adopted NCDS cohort felt similarly. Forty per cent of the study participants felt their health was excellent, compared to 26 per cent NCDS adopted women and 27 per cent in the main NCDS cohort.

As already mentioned, seven (10%) of the 72 women in our study, were considered to have a disability at the time of their adoption. Some of these conditions had been corrected before the children were placed for adoption. We found that, 40 years later, only two women (3%) considered themselves to have a disability and were registered disabled. These health problems had developed in later years and were unrelated to earlier recorded disabilities.

Fertility issues

We also gathered information on fertility and childbearing in our study participants. Is there any evidence of decreased fertility or any adverse or other effects on reproduction in these women who we believe received poor antenatal nutrition? Initial information from the women indicated that their average age of menarche was 13 years, compared with 13 years in the mid-1960s in the UK general population (Central Advisory Council for Education, 1967) and 12.5 to 13.25 years in southern Chinese girls in Hong Kong in the 1960s (Lee et al, 1963).

Fifty-one participants (71%) in our study had one or more children, including a small number of adopted children. However, 18 per cent reported problems with infertility, with 32 per cent informing us they had never been pregnant. For women born in 1960 in the UK the rate of childlessness is 19 per cent (Portanti and Whitworth, 2010). Childlessness can result from infertility or choice. Choice may include career development, or individual preferences, as well as many other factors.

The rate of childlessness in Hong Kong for a 1960 birth cohort is 22 per cent rising to 34 per cent for the 1965 birth cohort (Frejka et al, 2010). The reasons for this increase in childlessness in Hong Kong are related to social and economic factors. The rapid economic growth and demand for labour, together with lack of family-friendly work conditions and women being required to run households, bear and raise children and look after elderly parents, has delayed marriage and child bearing.

Although the childlessness rates for the women in our study are comparable with Hong Kong, the reasons are likely to differ. It has been speculated that poor nutrition in utero could affect future fertility. However, women exposed in utero to the Dutch famine of 1944–45 have been found to have more reproductive success than women not similarly exposed during foetal development (Painter et al, 2006).

Cultural/epidemiological/ ethnic differences

In recent times research has provided evidence that particular health problems are more prevalent in certain parts of the world. For example, we know that people from south-east China have an increased incidence of thalassaemia, hepatitis B, intolerance to alcohol (Aldehyde Dehydrogenase (ALDH) deficiency) and short-sightedness. This information may not have been widely available when women in our study were adopted in the 1960s.

Only one out of 72 women reported being a carrier for thalassaemia, which is far less than the expected incidence of 3.4 per cent having beta-thalassaemia and up to eight per cent having alpha or beta thalassaemia (Lau *et al*, 1997). This condition can remain undiagnosed as it is only significant if both parents are carriers of the trait and together could pass on a more serious condition to their offspring.

Four participants volunteered that they had hepatitis B (6%). The most likely route of infection is mother-to-child transmission. Current reports from China show the incidence of hepatitis B has been falling from a prevalence rate of 9.75% in 1992 (Dai and Qi, 1997) to seven per cent of the general population (Liang *et al*, 2005; Jia, 2008).

Two-thirds of the participants (66.7%) indicated that they had vision problems and the majority of these women were short-sighted or myopic. This is much higher than the incidence in the UK population (Logan *et al*, 2005) but comparable with national data for China, where 69.7 per cent of high school students are similarly affected (Xie *et al*, 2010).

Lifestyle choices

In recent decades, information about the health effects of lifestyle choices, such as smoking, drinking alcohol, type of diet and levels of exercise have been increasingly available. The importance of avoiding being overweight, or indeed underweight, has been emphasised. Government policies and health providers encourage people to take regular exercise and warn against the perils of smoking, taking illicit drugs and drinking alcohol to excess. Hence we were keen to find out about the women's lifestyle choices and the impact this has had on their general health and well-being. We included questions that allowed us to compare their habits with those of the matched UK-born groups in NCDS.

With regards to alcohol use, the study women's consumption was much lower than either of the NCDS comparison groups, as shown in Table 7.1. This could be linked with a condition known as aldehyde dehydrogenase (ALDH) deficiency (Goedde *et al*, 1984) – an enzyme deficiency which affects the body's ability to metabolise alcohol, and which is more common in certain ethnic groups, including Chinese people. It is very likely that some of our women found out early on

Table 7.1
Alcohol, smoking and exercise habits

	BCAS women (%) (n = 72)	NCDS non-adopted women (%) (n = 5, 115)	NCDS adopted women (%) (n = 50)
Alcohol			
– Have a drink most days	15	15	20
– 2–3 days a week	11	30*	28*
– Less often	50	49	48
– Never	24	6*	4*
Smoking			
– Never smoked	62	46*	32*
– Used to smoke but not now	23	25	26
– Smoke occasionally	6	4	0
– Smoke everyday	10	26*	42*
Exercise regularly (2–3 times a week or more)	63	43*	52

* On pairwise comparisons, these items all statistically significant from the BCAS responses (p < 0.05)

that they were unable to process alcohol and therefore avoided it. As one participant explained, 'I am actually allergic to alcohol. So I don't drink . . . I don't even touch it'.

The study women also reported much lower rates of smoking and higher rates of regular exercise (those who take part in exercise or physical activity 2–3 times a week). These positive lifestyle choices are likely to have an important impact in the longer term on health outcomes for the women.

Family health history

Adopted adults have often reported how frustrating it can be not to be able to answer questions about their family's health history when they visit their GP or attend hospital. Many value receiving information about family health history and knowing the implications this may have for themselves and their own children. Forty years ago, for children adopted within the UK, this information may not have been gathered as diligently as it is today. Family health history was often limited to birth mothers with little, if any, information on fathers. For the majority of the women in this study, the opportunity to obtain even basic medical information about the birth family was not and is not possible.

Not knowing about the birth family is a common area of concern:

It raised practical issues rather than emotional issues, which are still there today. When you are asked about your family medical history, basically I have got no idea what the family medical history is . . . In routine health screening questionnaires (concerning) heart disease . . . it's all very 'Yes' and 'No' and there is no 'I don't know' . . . that is what I worry about.

Conclusion

The specific health challenges that these women faced in their early lives do not seem to have adversely affected their general health and well-being over the long term. Some adult health conditions are more prevalent in this group as compared to UK-born groups by virtue of genetics, which would be the same for any Chinese woman today. Some of these conditions may not have been apparent or their heritability may have been unclear in previous years and perhaps issues were not identified or looked for as they would be today, for example, ALDH, thalassaemia and hepatitis B.

Analysis of the data collected from the questionnaires and at face-to-face interviews demonstrated no apparent increased risk of health problems and possibly fewer health conditions than one would have anticipated in view of these women's early experiences.

Comparisons between the study sample and the NCDS cohort, both adopted and non-adopted, are valuable, although as the incidence of some conditions was small, it has not been possible to test for differences in physical health outcomes. Comparisons between our sample and age-matched Chinese women with and without exposure to a similar early environment may have been more informative but was not possible.

However, we know that the risk of chronic health conditions associated with poor antenatal nutrition and being underweight at birth and in infancy can be modified by subsequent lifestyle changes. Participants in this study may well be demonstrating this. The significance of the higher rate of childlessness is unclear and requires further exploration to determine the relevance of infertility and choice.

It is also important to be mindful that institutional care is variable. The information we have collected would indicate a less adverse orphanage experience in Hong Kong when compared with other parts of the world. Following their adoption, throughout their childhoods, the girls in this study had access to universal healthcare, which would have contributed to the health outcomes reported here. Additionally, it is important to point out that in general the women have made lifestyle choices which further improve the likelihood of good health.

Summary

- Over half (55%) of the girls were noted to be slightly or moderately malnourished at examination prior to adoption. However, their health status was more positive than that of children from severely depriving institutions.
- We found no evidence of excessive health risk at follow-up for the conditions reported.
- Good nutrition and healthy lifestyle choices following adoption and into adulthood may have modified the risk of chronic poor health that can follow from early poor nutrition.
- Eighty-five per cent of participants described their own health as good or excellent, which was very similar to both NCDS comparison groups.

8 Belonging, difference and well-being

Introduction

One of the unique aspects of this study is that the participants were all ethnically Chinese women, adopted from overseas and, for the vast majority, placed transracially. We were conscious from the start that exploring the women's experience of intercountry and transracial adoption would be complex and an area that would be of great interest, particularly in view of the current UK policy initiatives to reduce the emphasis on ethnic matching in adoptive placements. This chapter reports on how the women described their experiences and how this relates to their well-being and the ways they chose to locate themselves socially.

The subject of transracial adoption, whether this results from children being placed in-country or internationally, has been controversial. Intercountry transracial adoption has raised many questions about the ethics and morality of removing children from developing countries to advanced and developed ones when children are the lifeblood of future generations. The counter-argument is that such placements are justified when there is no possibility of satisfactory care for children in their countries of origin. This rests on ensuring that children are "properly" available for adoption and not subject to trafficking or the exploitation of their parents.

Other concerns have centred on the "risks" to children born into a country with its own national identifications, history, ethnicities, culture, language and religions, and adopted into another. What does the child lose, or perhaps gain, when family, community and national characteristics are fundamentally different? Does what follows create such a powerful sense of alienation and difference that it seriously affects the child's development? How do children find ways of dealing with the potential for and realities of racist attitudes and discriminatory behaviour? Does a combination of these risk factors create hurdles that some transracially adopted children never overcome? Or are there positive factors that mitigate against any actual or potential harm, such as the effects of supportive adoptive parents who help their children counter discrimination?

At a different level, many questions have been asked about what ethnic and cultural identities actually mean when the child encounters "difference" on a daily basis. The concept of a personal and social identity is not limited to ethnic identity but includes other critical dimensions such as gender, sexuality, class, age, religion and, in the context of adoption, an adoptive identity. The idea that individuals develop a singular, unchanging identity has been recognised as seriously limiting and unhelpful. People have "identities" that are in varying degrees fluid and context specific. For any individual, identities are shaped by "lived experience" brought about through relational contexts – the internal sense of who somebody is, moderating and moderated by the significant people to whom they relate. This lived experience is expressed and reinforced through daily events, custom and practice, for example, preferred food, style of dress, taste in music, ceremonies and celebrations, level of education, prowess in sport, choice of leisure and how we function within the family unit; these are the means by which identity comes alive. This can and does change over time as individuals alter their perspective on who they are and the relational context of their lives change because they move school or leave home or develop a new set of relationships or live in a different community. As Gary Younge (2010, p 11) put it: 'The only thing certain about identity is that it will keep on changing'.

Individuals have compound identities where stability and change are ever-present dimensions. Stability and the sense of a "secure base" are often strongly "wished for" objectives in establishing identities. Social groups may exercise considerable pressure on individuals to maintain and aspire to ethnic, cultural, religious and language conformity of practice. This is often a particularly salient dimension of family life and the socialisation of children. It is also an important part of community experience – sometimes in a benign sense but in other cases with pressure to conform to prevailing values and norms. At the same time, opportunities to change and reject existing values and norms are common as children experience "different" values and norms at school and with peers or via the media. Adolescence in Western societies is typically associated with an opportunity to challenge and sometimes reject what went before as young people establish their own perspective on who they are and who they choose to be. The tensions and conflicts experienced during that period can be difficult, with the resolution extending well into early adulthood and beyond. As much as stable, secure base identities are something to be aspired to, change, conflict and challenge are likely to be an important part of the narrative of identity development. A cohesive sense of self is needed to manage these without undue psychological and social strain but it is unlikely that any individuals experience their identities without some degree of ongoing or transitional upset and upheaval.

Being Chinese in the UK

The study sample has grown up with two major reference groups: that of their adoptive home environment and community, largely white Anglo-Saxon, and those who share their broad Chinese genetic heritage, or perhaps individuals who have a South-East Asian appearance. A brief sketch of the UK Chinese population may be useful in understanding how these women locate themselves in the context of other Chinese people in the UK.

People of Chinese origin have arrived in the UK at different times and by different routes, mainly over the last 150 years. They came first of all as a result of the shipping trade from China and settled in the major ports, and later by reason of employment, education, seeking asylum or joining family members already living in the UK. In general, they have been economically successful and many have become well qualified. Although perhaps once associated with the catering and laundry industries, they now follow much more diverse occupations and professions. They range from new arrivals to those whose families have been in the UK for several generations.

The UK Chinese population comes mostly from Hong Kong,

Singapore and Malaysia, reflecting the history of British colonialism. The last reported census figures for the UK estimated that 247,403 people describing themselves as of Chinese origin were living the UK, forming 0.4 per cent of the total population (Office for National Statistics, 2005). They represent a fairly small minority group compared with Africans, Asians and African-Caribbean people. They reside mostly in England but also in Wales, Scotland and Northern Ireland (Modood and Berthoud, 1997).

Trying to describe the common characteristics of the Chinese population runs the risk of stereotyping, but it is of course with such stereotypes that they are so often confronted. One common and now possibly outdated view of the Chinese communities is that they tend to remain somewhat detached from those around them. However, the population is not uniform and will range from recently arrived manual workers to British-born, university-educated professionals. A further challenge to the idea of a segregated community is the fact that Chinese people are the most likely of all minority ethnic groups to marry someone of a different ethnicity to their own, true of a third of Chinese women (Modood and Berthoud, 1997). Within the mainstream media, there seem to be relatively few prominent British Chinese people active in politics, or popular entertainment but this may be a false picture in that a Chinese heritage is not always obvious or declared.

As with other visible minorities, to be seen as Chinese may subject the person to xenophobia, prejudice and discrimination. The most recent survey of the experiences of racism directed at Chinese communities in the UK found that such discriminatory treatment may be more prevalent than is generally known, due to under-reporting (Adamson et al, 2009). On the other hand, some of the attributes projected onto Chinese people include the positive stereotypes of being industrious and model citizens.

Belonging, difference and well-being for the BCAS women

The majority of the women in this study grew up in adoptive families with two white parents. Nine participants had one Chinese or part-Chinese adoptive parent. Eighteen of the women grew up with a sister also adopted from Hong Kong. Five women had at least one other sibling with a different Asian or minority ethnic heritage, most of whom were born in the UK.

The study's approach to assessing the women's views on identities and communities

Researching ethnicity in intercountry adoption is challenging. The consequences of being born in one part of the world and brought up by a family in another raises questions about the impact that fundamental differences might have during childhood, adolescence and adulthood on a secure and coherent sense of self with all of its psychological and social components. Measuring such concepts in a valid and significant way is hard to achieve, given the conceptual complexities identified above.

The questionnaire pack included three sets of questions devised specifically for the study focusing on the particular circumstances of these women. They were:

1. Connectedness to UK Chinese communities and culture
2. Connectedness to UK society
3. Chinese appearance

The responses are presented in full in the tables. In addition to the questionnaires, the interviews covered childhood experiences including within the adoptive family, experiences at school and in the wider community. Other interview questions focused on adult experiences and reflections on topics like ethnic self-identification, appearance, connectedness to the Chinese and British communities in the UK, experiences of racism and stereotyping and how these were dealt with.

We saw this as an exploratory investigation to understand better the responses of our participants rather than as an attempt to devise and test new scales in terms of demonstrated reliability and validity. It was not necessarily our intention to recommend the following indices for use on broader samples.

Self-described ethnic/national identity: Which box do I tick?

The 2001 census in the UK was the first to collect self-reported ethnic categorisation. Many other data collection tools used a similar form of categorisation from employment application forms to a wide range of survey data. For internationally and transracially adopted adults, this seemingly straightforward exercise may be more complex. Most of the forms used for such purposes only allow responses within standardised pre-set categories. One participant (Erica) pointed out that being labelled as "non-white other" is neither a helpful nor a welcome description. We wanted to find out how these women choose to describe their own ethnic identity.

Of the 72 women, 50 per cent described their ethnic identity as Chinese, 19 per cent as British and 15 per cent as British Chinese. Less common responses (two or fewer each) were Chinese British, British Asian, half-Chinese, half-English and white British. One woman said that she sometimes ignores the question and sometimes selects Chinese, while for another, the question raises such complex and painful issues that she tries, if at all possible, to avoid answering it. Only two participants regularly speak a language other than English at home, and in both cases these women were living in other European countries and spoke the local language.

Connectedness to Chinese communities and UK society

As described earlier, we developed scales for this study to measure connectedness to the Chinese communities in the UK and to wider UK society. This was in order to ascertain to what extent these internationally and transracially adopted women had a sense of belonging, felt comfortable in their social context, and had established links to Chinese communities. The responses to all items are presented in Table 8.1.

Table 8.1
Connectedness to Chinese communities and culture

Connectedness to Chinese communities and culture	*Strongly agree/ agree %*	*Strongly disagree/ disagree %*	*Factor*
1. I have close friends who have Chinese origins	19	81	1
2. I regularly socialise with other Chinese people	14	86	1
3. I know people of Chinese origin in my local community	29	71	1
4. I take an active interest in Chinese culture (its history, traditions, customs)	46	54	2
5. I am active in organisations or social groups attended mostly by Chinese people	7	93	1
6. I prefer to be in the company of other Chinese people	3	97	1
7. I actively seek to make connections with the UK Chinese community	4	96	1
8. I have representations of Chinese culture in my home (e.g. Chinese decorations/ornaments/pictures/music)	4	96	2
9. I observe customs around Chinese New Year	4	96	2
10. I have tried to learn Chinese (any dialect)	25	75	1
11. I am able to speak and/or read Chinese (any dialect)	6	94	1

Factors derived from the scale were:
Factor 1 "Social" – (8 items) was labelled "active socialising with other Chinese people"
Factor 2 "Cultural" (3 items) was labelled "Strong Chinese cultural interest and identity"

In relation to connectedness to Chinese communities, nearly 20 per cent of the sample reported that they had close friends or regularly socialised with other people of Chinese origin but very few were members of organisations attended mainly by Chinese people, preferred the company of other Chinese people or actively sought to make connections with Chinese communities (7% or less for each item). A quarter had tried to learn Chinese (usually Mandarin or Cantonese) but only a few had reached any level of fluency. A much higher proportion (46%) reported taking an active interest in Chinese culture (its history, traditions, and customs).

Individual items from the "connectedness to UK society" scale indicate that regular local socialising was common and virtually all felt comfortable in public places in the UK (see Table 8.2 below). The majority agreed that they felt a sense of belonging in Britain and were comfortable with being described as British Chinese, although this term had different meanings for different people. In an item asking about cultural identity, half of the sample (49%) thought of themselves as having more than one cultural identity.

Table 8.2
Connectedness to UK society index

Connectedness to UK society index	Strongly agree/ agree %	Strongly disagree/ disagree %
1. I feel a sense of "belonging" within British society	86	14
2. I regularly talk to my neighbours	86	14
3. I regularly socialise with people in my local area	72	28
4. I generally feel comfortable going out to public places (like restaurants, wine bars, pubs, parks or cafés)	98	2
5. I feel comfortable describing myself as British	86	14
6. I think of myself as British/Chinese	82	18

We compared the answers given on these two scales with the women's interview responses for each individual case. For the majority of the women, the fuller explanations and examples they gave in their interviews broadly supported their questionnaire responses: for example, those who emphasised their Chinese origins as being important to them tended to have answered positively to the items on the "connectedness to Chinese communities scale". However, given the limited number of questionnaire items, we found evidence of a number of other ways in which women chose to express affiliation with Chinese communities and cultural practices. Examples included talking to their children about their early experiences to try and instil a sense of pride in their Chinese heritage, or watching TV programmes and films about Hong Kong and China.

A key question is whether those people who describe only a loose connection with their ethnic group display difficulties in other areas of psychological and social functioning. We used the data from the "connectedness to Chinese communities" scale to test whether a low score on this index was associated with poorer outcomes on measures of psychological and social functioning or life satisfaction. Tests were carried out for any associations between the 11-item connectedness index (for details, see Table 8.1) and the following well-being measures: GHQ, Malaise inventory, Rosenberg Self-esteem Questionnaire, Mental Health Consultation Index and Life Satisfaction scale (taken from NCDS, 2004) and GAF scales (as described in Chapter 4).

We found that, for this group of women, a low score on connectedness to Chinese communities does not show a statistically significant relationship (using t-tests, and Fischer's exact test for GAF) with elevated risks on indicators of psychological well-being and life satisfaction. This suggests that, although the majority of the women in this study did not describe themselves as having developed close links with either Chinese people in the UK or an active engagement with Chinese cultural activities or interests, this was not found to be associated with difficulties in psychological and social functioning.

As we know from the findings presented in Chapter 4, as a group these women showed no higher risk of mental health problems than our comparison groups of UK-born women; in other words, our group had a similar proportion of women who had poorer mental health outcomes.

It could plausibly be argued that mental health questionnaires may not capture all of the psychological reactions to stresses such as those outlined in this chapter. However, the measures we selected do cover a range of important areas of well-being. These include everyday worries and feelings of anxiety, reactions to stress, such as sleeping problems or loss of appetite, and feelings of low self-worth. We also examined whether psychological difficulties reached a level where the women have sought professional help. The link between community connectedness and well-being was therefore important to test although these findings should be considered alongside the responses from the interviews rather than in isolation.

Chinese appearance

The third scale comprised seven questions on Chinese appearance including three "pairs" of items about the differences between childhood and the present. In the interviews most women described feeling increasingly comfortable over time with being identified as Chinese in appearance. For some this was a gradual shift as they passed through adolescence and into an independent adult life with more choice over where to live and with whom to spend time. But for others this was a more painful process and one that seemed to throw up confusing and painful experiences that were not within their control.

The responses to the questionnaire items are presented in Table 8.3. Eighty-eight per cent of the women described themselves as feeling comfortable with their Chinese appearance. This was in comparison with 44 per cent who felt comfortable when they were growing up. During childhood, 75 per cent of the women had at times wished to look less Chinese but this had reduced to 19 per cent by the time of the survey. When asked how comments about the fact that they looked different from their adoptive family had affected them, 54 per cent said this made them feel uncomfortable when they were growing up and 29 per cent still found this to be the case.

Table 8.3
Chinese appearance

Chinese appearance	When growing up (agreed or strongly agreed with statement)	Now (agreed or strongly agreed with statement)
I was/am comfortable with my Chinese appearance	44%	88%
I wish(ed) at times to look less Chinese	75%	19%
Comments about looking different from my adoptive family make/made me feel uncomfortable	54%	29%
Because of my appearance, I feel uncomfortable in certain situations in the UK	–	43%

McNemar tests show that changes in first three pairs of statements are all highly significant (p <0.001).

The responses suggest a growing sense of feeling at ease with their appearance – both looking Chinese and looking different from other members of their adoptive family – a finding that was also apparent in many of the individual interviews. However, this is not the full story: 43 per cent of the sample agreed or strongly agreed that there were certain experiences where they felt uncomfortable because of their Chinese appearance: examples included being the only Chinese person in a professional environment, going to pubs in rural areas, or facing groups of children making racist comments. As has already been noted, identity is both complex and multi-factional, and the descriptions given by the study sample clearly reflect how that works in reality.

Interview data on Chinese appearance
Variations in experiences in childhood and adulthood – and reactions to such experiences – were explored in greater depth in the interviews.

149

Some women linked specific events, such as getting married, having children or developing a career, to a growing sense of ease and a corresponding increase in feeling more comfortable with their Chinese appearance. Although most of these participants chose to describe any experiences of racism or prejudice as relatively low-level, this group also included women who had experienced regular race-based bullying during childhood. However, for some, this shift to a more positive view had been hard won and they could recall specific, painful incidents of racist or discriminatory comments. These were often reported with caveats, such as how times had changed for the better.

For those who expressed discomfort with their Chinese appearance in both childhood and adulthood, the effects on their lives varied. Some described this as a negative but not hugely significant factor, while for a minority of women being reminded of their Chinese appearance was consistently painful. The woman quoted below was not alone in her view that feeling different and experiencing racism and prejudice continues to be a burden that will never go away.

I hate it because I feel English, I think English, and I think of myself as English but I don't look it . . . the first thing they do is treat you like an outsider . . . so it means I can't really fit in. It means you are marked out, you can't be unobtrusive. Faith

A small group of individuals described these experiences as having had a substantial negative impact on their well-being. Some women reported that their children had also experienced race-based bullying based on their appearance. They gave examples of how they tried to acknowledge these insults and act protectively. One had helped her young child to explain to a classmate where Hong Kong was in a positive way, while another recalled her daughter enjoying moving to London where she felt able to blend into a more multicultural environment.

Looking outward versus the way others see you

In addition to the themes explored in the indices developed for this study, we asked the women to elaborate on their experiences. A common theme was contrasting how the world appeared, looking out on it from the inside, and how they believe they are seen by others. Everyday occurrences could be a reminder of "difference"; for example, other people could be surprised when they spoke with a regional UK accent and appear confused when meeting for the first time without foreknowledge of their Chinese appearance.

When people first meet me they think I am Chinese, but as soon as I open my mouth they know that I am Scottish bred . . . I don't realise that I look Chinese. I get surprised every single time . . . when either somebody Chinese comes up and starts speaking Chinese to me, or else I am getting racial abuse and I am thinking – why? It is something that my brain has never taken on board. Moira

One participant voiced an idea that others touched on but found difficult to express.

It is not my appearance that I feel uncomfortable with and I don't remember a time of feeling uncomfortable . . . it is the things that go with it. You look Chinese but you don't have a Chinese upbringing or background – can't speak the language, that sort of thing. So there's a kind of disconnect. Celia

Some felt that other Chinese people could tell by their mannerisms or looks that they were not culturally Chinese. Not all the participants were living in the UK and some gave examples of how they saw themselves and how they were seen once they had left.

Growing up wanting to be the same ethnicity as their adoptive family was only mentioned explicitly by a few participants, and in most cases was felt to have been a childhood phase:

I think the only thing about being Chinese is that you always want what you don't have and you always think I'd like to be

blonde with blue eyes and big eyes and not sort of small little eyes, and you always want to be different . . . but you know it's not like you can have plastic surgery and you can change yourself. When I was at college and I started working in London, there were some people that found me quite attractive and I thought, oh well, that's quite nice actually . . . in fact, sometimes it had benefitted me because I . . . was not blue-eyed and blonde. Marion

Becoming aware of ethnic and cultural differences

For many participants, growing up in a white family meant that it was only when someone else drew attention to their noticeable difference in appearance that they became aware of it. Starting school therefore could often call attention to an issue that they had previously never thought about.

Before you go to primary school when you are very small you are enveloped in a bubble, very protected, and you actually don't know that you are different . . . You can't see your own face when you are little . . . and when you look outwards, everybody looks different. So it is only when people point it out to you that that is when you know. And obviously, unless you have got nasty parents, they have always protected you. So you are not aware of it until you are about five when you go to school. Celia

For others this awareness occurred even later, after leaving home or moving to a new environment.

I used to almost forget that I was Chinese – that sounds a bit bizarre but I suppose being surrounded by so many white people as such, but I think now, where I work in a community where there's a large number of Chinese people, I look at them and I think . . . I almost think, do I look like that too? It is quite strange in a way – I mean my sisters are half-Chinese so it's not like they're white. Caroline

Several participants described that even today, now in their 40s or 50s, how they think of themselves differs from how others see them.

I have never really seen myself as non-white. Someone would say, have you looked in a mirror lately? But it doesn't bother me because I know I have got so many friends who are non-white and at any given time when I am working, the shifts will be made up of mostly Filipinos and people from Africa. And if they are white they are probably from Ireland. So they are not English. I think it is fascinating. Vivian

Explaining difference early on in a new situation

Several participants could recall from childhood that their parents found themselves having to explain their relationship to others at an early stage in new situations. Some viewed this as positive – that their visible difference led to open discussions and therefore talking about being adopted lost any sense of sensationalism.

I think it had to be talked about because I looked different. By the time I was going to school, I looked different to absolutely everybody else in the very small village that we lived in . . . I mean, I just didn't know anybody that looked like me. I don't remember any big deal about it; it was just part of normal life. Erica

In other cases, however, overhearing these explanations was a cause for confusion or hurt.

I do remember quite vividly when my dad, when I was younger and they had a dinner party and I had come down for water and to see what was going on, and he introduced me as his 'adopted daughter' which really shocked me because again the use of 'adoption' but also the fact that he was saying that I was his 'adopted daughter' rather than his daughter. So that hit me quite hard. Janice

153

A common experience was the sense that, when meeting someone for the first time, their accent and name would lead others to assume that they were white British. Often these situations arose at work, and one participant, Lynn, recalled that her mother had always told her to send a photograph with job applications so that when she turned up for interviews there would not be "any awkwardness".

In most cases this was seen as a nuisance rather than offensive, and some participants felt that assumptions about others are easy to make.

I'm not consciously aware of being Chinese. The only times are like, if you've spoken to someone on the phone, and they say, 'Shall we meet up?' or whatever, and they don't know what you look like. Sometimes I can think, 'Ooh, they're going to think of somebody white and English'. Most times they might say, 'Oh I didn't expect . . .' but you know, because I hadn't explained. Jackie

School
Like many children who look different from their peers, some women hated having their difference in appearance highlighted when they wished to blend in with other children. The task of having to explain themselves to others started early and was often life-long. One of the first experiences was in primary school when they had to explain their adoptive status to other children when their parent(s) arrived to pick them up. Many examples were given of racist taunting and bullying such as objects and paint being thrown, name calling such as being called "slit eyes" and "Chinky". Chinese accents were mimicked and repeated jokes about Chinese restaurant menu numbers became tedious. Although many of the incidents included specific racist elements, some reported feeling that such experiences were more universal.

I am quite comfortable with it as an adult. I wasn't as a child because . . . I used to get called names and things. But now I am adult and I realise that kids would call you names whatever you

are, it doesn't seem so bad. But at the time it is awful, isn't it?
Carol

Taunting and bullying can of course be perpetrated on the basis of other characteristics, for example, poverty, disability or even hair colour. Many of the women pointed out that they were well aware of other children being the subject of hostility for a range of reasons and that their ethnic origins were not the only form of difference to attract attention.

While I was still there (in grammar school) I deliberately tried not to have a posh accent because you could be picked on by children from other schools for having a posh accent, or they could see your school uniform and you would be picked on for that . . . Ellen

Almost all of the participants could recall incidents of name-calling, and while some brushed this off, others recalled how difficult this had been. Looking back as adults, many felt that their parents had not known what to do, rather than being unaware or deliberately ignoring the problem.

You know it was hard and I told my mum about it but she really wasn't able to help me because she did not understand what it was like . . . Everything was a first experience for our family going through all this. And she did go and talk to the headmaster, but I mean, how are you going to handle that? Even for the school it was a first because I was the first foreigner there. Rita

Others made a conscious decision not to tell their parents about it and many adopters were told of adverse incidents only once they escalated, for example, a thrown brick causing broken glasses.

A lot of the experiences I had as a child growing up with racism and stuff like that, I wouldn't tell [my mum], partly because you learn very quickly as a child that you don't respond. You know, people shout a racist remark . . . what they want is they want to

see you cry. They want to see you react. And I learned very
quickly and very soon that it was best to turn your back on it.
Katy

In a few cases, women could recall negative remarks coming not from peers but from staff members at school as in the example below.

In primary school my teacher stood me up in front of the class
one day and asked me a question on maths and I couldn't
answer it. And she said, 'Well, if you can't speak English you
shouldn't be here'. So of course I went back home and told Mum
and Mum was down there straight away . . . I can always
remember that, and I was only about six or seven at the time.
Eva

Although few could recall receiving strong support from staff at their schools, many women were quick to point out that awareness of diversity and anti-bullying policies would be much more common in schools today. Some gave examples based on their own experience as parents.

Parents or other adults were not the only source of potential support in dealing with bullying at school. Several participants reported that older siblings, especially those who attended the same school, helped them to deal with racist taunts. Sometimes this involved directly intervening and confronting those responsible, but in other cases their mere presence acted as a deterrent. Paula, who grew up in a large family of mixed ethnicity, explained.

There must have been problems but because we were a group,
you know, it is like pick on one and you pick on everybody. So I
think we all sort of ignored them and I think we just carried on
doing what we wanted to.

Others who felt able to shrug off the bullying put this down to having close friends or other good experiences at school. This provided a balance that reduced the impact of the incidents.

Life in the adoptive home

One of the key findings on transracial placements has been the potential for dislocation of ethnic, cultural and religious group membership and identities and the possible implications that this might have throughout childhood and adulthood for developing a coherent and cohesive sense of belonging and connectedness. More recently, adopters have been encouraged to make links with the country or community of origin in order for the growing child to feel an ease of identification and connection. Such attempts, however, can be experienced in isolation rather than as part of the lived experience of everyday life. Celia noted the difference between "learning about" culture and building relationships with people:

We were taken to exhibitions and things when we were kids and I think they were trying . . . like when they had the Chinese Emperor, the Chinese soldiers, that kind of thing, they would make an effort to take me to things like that, but what I didn't have was any kind of contact with any Chinese community. It was mainly about looking at Chinese art.

One participant was told to feel proud to be Chinese but said her family didn't do anything to make her feel proud of her origins.

As other studies have found (see, for example, Tessler *et al*, 1999), the best efforts of adopters to encourage Chinese identification were met with resistance in adolescence when "difference" was too uncomfortable to be acknowledged or when other interests were more important. For example, Georgina's parents offered the opportunity of Cantonese lessons.

And I'm thinking, 'Do I want to go to school on a Saturday and learn a foreign language? No I don't think so, I'd rather go horse riding with my friends' so that was a no (laughter) . . . maybe if it had been dressed up slightly differently: 'Would you like to do some activities?' and included eating food, then I might have been more interested, but as it was, 'Would you like to go to lessons on a Saturday?' it didn't go down very well!

For most of the women, there was only very occasional contact with other Chinese children and families, even among some families with one Chinese parent. A small number of women reported that their families had taken in Chinese students as lodgers, or that their parents had friends in Hong Kong who would occasionally visit. There were a few families who set out deliberately to make Chinese friends, as was the case with Josephine.

They tried to find the nearest link with Chinese people . . . in those days in the 60s there weren't many ethnic people (sic) wandering around. So they took us down to the Chinese restaurant where we became incredibly good friends with the boys that ran the restaurant. And through those boys, we learnt to use chopsticks, become familiar with Chinese phrases, hearing Chinese voices and the language . . . When I was in my 20s I went to a Chinese restaurant in Chinatown with a boyfriend and they gave him a plate and a knife and fork and they gave me a bowl and chopsticks. And as it happened, it didn't faze me because I had used them before because my parents had done that.

The women expressed mixed feelings on whether more opportunities would have been helpful in retrospect. Describing their thoughts, participants often referred to the issue being raised when others asked questions.

I saw myself as half-European because of my upbringing. So that is how blurred my identity is. Because I have always had to explain how I was brought up and I don't speak Chinese. And everyone says it is a shame I have lost the language and I felt kind of bad about that as well, almost guilty that I had not kept up my Chinese. Well, how would I have kept up my Chinese? My family didn't establish the means by which I could have done that. Sophie

For some women, the sense of lacking links to their origins was described as an ongoing preoccupation.

The large portion of what makes me who I am is what is missing and that became more of a hole as I got older because there are things you need to have reassured, whether that is through the social mirror or through parental or antecedent whatever . . . Irrespective of who you are, whether you acknowledge it or not, it becomes actually a very important thing in relationship to what has gone before and what may come . . . If you don't have those reflections back, even in a simplistic way like in popular media, how do you put yourself into the society that you are supposed to slot into? Victoria

These feelings of disjuncture, although powerful in many cases, were by no means universal. The extent to which forging connections with Chinese communities or identifying with particular cultural practices was seen as a central concern varied. Erica described her adoptive family as "colour-blind" and felt this had served her well.

What I haven't done is go chasing off to a big cosmopolitan area to go looking or to go searching for people that are like me or people that are from the same ethnicity, and it doesn't interest me . . . I sort of think that intercountry adoptions nowadays would be very carefully and skillfully managed so all this didn't happen, but for me it worked. There are big gaps in my cultural identity but I don't feel the poorer for it. I might have been richer if I had had it, I don't know. But I don't really feel that I'm bereft of anything.

All of the women bar one knew the Chinese name they had been given, usually by orphanage staff. Around a third (n = 22) use their Chinese name in some way, most commonly as a middle name retained in full or in part by their adoptive parents. Some of these women choose to use both their first and middle names regularly while others include only their middle name if filling in official forms.

Reactions to and strategies for coping with racism

One participant recounted that, on the first day at primary school, a boy spat in her face and told her to go back home. She followed this quickly with: 'But not all the kids were doing this and it was not ongoing'. Reactions to racist insults varied from taking a robust stance: 'You either sink under it or toughen it out – and that's what I did' or keeping out of the way of the offender: 'not very noble' as one person put it. Some women regretted that their adoptive parents were not more active in tackling racial abuse with the school authorities.

Adopters often responded by telling the children to ignore the insults, but this was frequently not felt to be sufficient. Other parents were more likely to be vocal in challenging racism, and this was not necessarily linked to closeness to adoptive parents. One participant commented that this was prior to the introduction of anti-bullying policies and such things would these days be taken up in her daughters' school. One mother used racist remarks to her – allegedly to toughen her up!

Coping with racism and prejudice in adulthood

The changes in British society and the growing ethnic diversity of the population are well-documented, although the way that this has changed racist attitudes and behaviour at personal and institutional level, is much less clear. The women in this group are not immune from racist abuse and harassment even today in urban, multicultural environments as well as elsewhere. Not all of the examples of racism were from white people nor did they all occur in the UK.

The most common experiences as adults were of racial abuse in the street, which tended to be isolated comments from strangers 'usually by a young idiot'. One participant commented: 'I've got a standard reply now to people who call out, I just tell them to grow up.' While some women described this as a rare occurrence and a passing nuisance, at the other extreme end were reports of physical threats or actual harm.

Some descriptions reflected a keenness deliberately to categorise isolated racist remarks as minor incidents, which they did their best to laugh off rather than let it affect them: 'To me it's water off a duck's back' or 'I let it go in one ear and out the other'. In the face of prejudice some described the hurt as somewhat attenuated when others were supportive.

As described earlier, almost 90 per cent of the participants who were in relationships had a white European partner. Eighty-two per cent of the women reported that they had never had a Chinese partner. Most relationships with partners' families were described as problem-free and in some cases a source of valued support. There were, however, isolated examples of prejudice, where partners' parents had reacted negatively to the relationship in the early stages or had made insulting jokes in front of the women. More common were reports that ultimately their ethnic heritage had little effect on these relationships.

Work

Sometimes discrimination operated more subtly at work. When the prejudice was openly expressed, some women dealt with this directly, for example, confronting the person involved and firmly stating that such behaviour was unacceptable. Some experiences, however, were much harder to pin down or prove and, in such cases, not knowing how to proceed usually made the problem difficult to confront. The most common experiences involved either having racist remarks directed at them, usually by customers rather than colleagues, or over-hearing such comments while at work. The women gave mixed reports of managers' or senior colleagues' treatment of such issues and whether this had led to them feeling supported or further undermined. In a small number of cases, women felt that the stereotypes of Chinese women being quiet and polite could be helpful.

It was notable that participants strived to be balanced and con-sidered in accounting for any unjust treatment. They objected to the insults, but qualified this with noting when this was an isolated occur-rence and not sustained. They shaped their responses with caveats – slurs were not always seen as seriously malicious and not everyone held hostile views. Even those who had experienced overt prejudice wanted to counter-balance this with reporting that others showed genuine interest in them as individuals. Some wished to refrain from blaming their parents and school and explained that a transracial adoption was 'an unknown thing at the time' – but added that there was no excuse for ignorance now.

Some women pointed out that such experiences were less common in adulthood, although it was not always clear why this was the case.

I think racism diminishes as you get older but that's also sort of a feminist issue, isn't it? I mean you become less visible as you get older, and so a lot of the racism that I experienced in this country has gone and that's partly a change in the political climate but I also think it's because I've got older, because racism is often very mixed up with sexism, which comes from young men, so they see a woman and they're having a go on two counts. Georgina

Identifications by self and others

As noted earlier, the construction of ethnicity for these participants was a complex process. Being of Chinese origin and raised in the UK frequently resulted in false assumptions about the person's history. A common example was being spoken to in Cantonese in Chinese restaurants and having to explain that they could not speak the language.

How other people, especially strangers, reacted to them was an ongoing source of disquiet for many. Questioning about origins was sometimes experienced as aggressive and unwelcome – but at other times as just benign curiosity. Some were pleased with their growing assertiveness in the face of unthinking assumptions: 'They used to say, "Oh, do your mum and dad own the local Chinese restaurant?" or whatever, and I used to say, "No, I'm adopted"' (Maxine). One participant enjoyed confounding the European stereotype of Chinese females being quiet and shy by being naturally loud and outspoken.

Here is an example of tackling the question of self-identification when dealing not with a singular but with a compound identity:

I would describe myself as Chinese in terms of where I originated from, but I don't describe myself as a Chinese person because I don't really feel like that. So I suppose I'm English, but then I don't think that I'm fully English. I don't know. It's difficult to explain really. Maureen

By no means was everyone in conflict about how they identified themselves or wanting to identify with white people: 'I never had any hang-ups about who I was. It never occurred to me that I'd want to be anything different.' Some explained that they felt English and happily led what they considered to be a typically British way of life.

For some, there were even upsides to others' assumptions.

Some people assume you can't speak Chinese, otherwise they assume you speak Chinese and you can't speak English. A lot of the time I say, 'Pardon? What did you say?' And they go, 'Oh, she understands me.' But then I have been able to take it to my advantage sometimes when I have done something silly, I can just look innocent, I am Chinese, I don't understand you. It works that way so I have played on that a little bit. Jane

I think in some ways it was probably to my advantage because being a female and, you know, more likely to be noticed. For instance, at a party or something, people always say, 'Ooh yes I saw you,' and I think, 'I never saw you!' and it is only because I think you are slightly different from everyone else and so people notice you more, and so later on people will say, 'Yeah, I remember seeing you,' and you think, 'Ah, but I never saw you'. Paula

Conclusion

We have presented the diverse range of views of a group of women who share similar early experiences but whose lives since adoption have followed individual pathways. The quantitative scales developed for this study allowed us to begin to unravel the relationships between their self-regard, connectedness to Chinese communities and wider UK society, and overall well-being.

Reviewing all of the qualitative and quantitative data collected for our study about identities and communities, we draw four main conclusions. First, when asked in a free-response item how they usually choose to describe their own ethnicity, half of the participants said Chinese, 19 per cent said British and 15 per cent said British Chinese. They saw themselves as both British (by nationality and cultural socialisation) and Chinese (by genetic inheritance). This expression of a dual identification was common but not true for all. When asked to respond to the questionnaire item 'I feel comfortable describing myself as British', 86 per cent agreed that this was the case. We conclude from this that there is little evidence of this group of women choosing to disavow either a British or Chinese identity.

Second, given the proposition that feelings of not belonging and marginality in transracial samples can lead to serious psychological distress, we chose to measure community connectedness (UK and Chinese) via newly devised questionnaires and follow-up interview questions. We then tested the relationship between the "connectedness to Chinese communities" index and psychological well-being. We found no evidence for associations between higher connectedness to Chinese communities and/or affiliation with Chinese cultural practices and mental well-being in adulthood, or between connectedness and worse mental health.

The issue of whether a link existed between ethnic identity development and psychological well-being has been comprehensively reviewed (Castle *et al*, 2011). This review showed that a variety of concepts had been utilised, including ethnic identity (often using Phinney's Multigroup Ethnic Identification Measure), parents' socialisation of their transracially adopted children, ethnic pride and sense of difference. The findings did not prove to be consistent in evidencing such links, making it difficult to draw strong conclusions. As the authors note, there is a lack of quantitative studies and reliable, valid measures developed so far. All bar one of the studies reviewed were carried out in the US, and the sole UK research concerned adolescents in residential care (Robinson, 2000). Further research with UK adopted populations would prove informative.

Third, our data, particularly the interviews, showed how distressing and perturbing various aspects of some of these women's lives have been and/or continue to be. For example, some had felt alienated, struggled with conflicts of dual/multiple identities and had experienced race-based mistreatment. The interview narratives highlighted some common experiences of childhood growing up from the 1960s onwards in different locations in the UK, particularly in relation to dealing with varying levels of racism, prejudice and feelings of belonging and difference within their adoptive families and wider communities. By adulthood, most women appear to have found ways with which to deal with such experiences adequately, but there was consistent evidence that being forced to deal with others' assumptions was problematic for some of the women.

Although research is scant, there is one recent study focusing on the incidences of racism directed at the UK Chinese population (Adamson *et al*, 2009). This report goes into great detail about a variety of experiences, including harassment and violence. The study women's reports of verbal abuse and, less frequently, physical attacks are in line with these findings. No reports of destruction of property were made in our sample, which differs from Adamson *et al*'s survey of a wider population of Chinese men and women.

Fourth, we found that the women were much less likely in adulthood to report feeling uncomfortable at times with their Chinese appearance than in their childhood. This could be related to their own psychological development over time and/or the changing social context of these women's lives, including partners, families and other social relationships through work or where they chose to live.

In reporting on questions of identities and psychological adjustments, we regard both of these aspects as equally important. A divergence of views on whether one carries more weight than the other is true for our participants as well as for commentators in this contested field. Within a society such as ours, where physical difference is constantly noted and the assumptions that arise from this have a direct impact on the everyday lives of individuals, a scientific enquiry is not able to resolve this issue in which value positions are so prominent.

Looking back at life as well as thinking about present experience, when this stretches over 40 years or so, is likely to confront any individual with a complex set of thoughts, feelings and perspectives on who they are and what brought this about. Doing so is a subjective process that combines hopes, fears, disappointments and achievements. As with other research, measuring outcomes is not free of value judgements. Is it sufficient to argue that because things turned out well, previous bad experiences were not as bad as they seemed at the time? These issues are very salient for this study, as has been identified at various points. They are also important questions when thinking about the implications of the study's findings when there are serious questions raised about matching children, when adoption is their plan, with adopters who can reflect and/or can promote their ethnic identity.

Since these intercountry adoptions took place, some 50 years ago, "same race" placements as the strongly preferred option have come to dominate practice in UK domestic adoptions. In the late 1990s, there was increasing concern that the pursuit of such practice was causing delay to children from minority ethnic backgrounds, with some never being placed in a family because such a match could not be found. Subsequent legislation requires adoption agencies and the courts to give due consideration to 'a child's religious persuasion, racial origin and cultural and linguistic background' but to balance these considerations against the duty to avoid delay in placing the child. These issues continue to challenge those involved in adoption. Evaluating the complex range of issues that are present without allowing one issue to dominate, but at the same time not being seen to ignore it, requires considerable maturity, understanding and insight.

The personal accounts of the women in relation to racism and discrimination are disturbing. The absence of help and the lack of understanding in many instances are also deeply troubling. But equally notable is the creativity, resilience and presence of support in rising to the challenge of these experiences. It is also striking to hear the adjustments that were made in developing a strong and secure sense of identity in relation to their appearance, connection and sense of membership to the people and communities around them.

The development of meaningful identities over the life course is undoubtedly complex. For many women, the conflicts, uncertainties and stresses of those processes have not gone away but they have not come to dominate their lives in a way that is indicated through standardised measures of health, mental health or other enduring adverse problems. That is a very important finding but it is not an excuse for some of what happened along the way. The findings from this study are testament to both the insidious nature of racism and discrimination in the UK and resilience in the face of it.

Summary

- Half of the participants identified themselves as Chinese, 19% said British and 15% said British Chinese and the remainder used less common definitions. Generally speaking, they saw themselves as both British (by nationality and cultural socialisation) and Chinese (by genetic inheritance).
- Most women felt comfortable being described as British Chinese and the majority also agreed that they felt a sense of belonging in the UK.
- We found no evidence on our statistical tests for associations between higher connectedness to Chinese communities and/or affiliation with Chinese cultural practices and mental well-being in adulthood, or between connectedness and worse mental health.
- Interview data gave illustrations of feelings of alienation and struggles with conflicts of dual/multiple identities and experiences of race-based mistreatment.
- The women were much less likely in adulthood to report feeling uncomfortable at times with their Chinese appearance than in their childhood.

- The conflicts, uncertainties and stresses of identification processes have not gone away over the lifespan but for most women they have not come to dominate their lives in terms of psychological well-being.

9　Origins and access to information

Introduction

As noted in Chapter 5, the vast majority of the women in the study had been "abandoned", usually to be quickly found by passers-by. This meant that they had no information about why their parents had felt unable to care for them or of their family background. For the few that were relinquished, the information was limited. These factors underline just how different the context of these women's adoptions is from those adopted people born and adopted in the UK, the majority of whom would nowadays have access to information about their origins.

In the UK the right of adopted people to have access to information about their origins is well established and all countries in the UK have legislation that allows adopted people to receive information enabling them to obtain a copy of their original birth certificate.[18] The legislative framework recognises that adoption is a life-long process and that it is important to give adopted people the opportunity to gain access to information if they want to learn more about their origins and seek answers to the questions they may have.

For many adopted people, obtaining a copy of an original birth certificate is often the springboard that enables them to gather more information about their origins and begin a search for birth family members if they so wish. Over the past few decades there has been a great deal of interest in understanding what makes some adopted people seek to access information and then search for birth relatives, whilst others apparently show no interest. A number of research

---

18 The need for adopted people to have access to information about their origins was recognised when the Children Act 1975 came into force. This gave adopted people in England and Wales the right, once they reached the age of 18 years, to obtain the necessary information to get a copy of their original birth certificate. This had always been a right for people adopted in Scotland as the 1930 Act addressed this at the time. In Northern Ireland it became a right in 1987.

studies have examined this intriguing question (Triseliotis, 1973; Sachdev, 1989; Rozenburg and Groze, 1997; Howe and Feast, 2000). Muller and Perry (2001a) reviewed one hundred studies that had been undertaken in different countries on the subject of search and reunion, the majority conducted in the US. They recognised that some of these studies had limitations due to the samples being small and unrepresentative, but they concluded that there were three theoretical models with regard to searching that emerge from the literature review. These are:

1. The psychopathological model – attributing the adopted person's desire to search to some personal deficiencies or the malfunctioning of the adoptive family
2. The normative model – the search for information about origins is a normal process: a developmental task the adopted person needs to undertake as part of their psychosocial development
3. the social-interactionist model – places the adopted person's search within the context of socio-cultural norms and expectations, suggesting that searching is a reaction of adoptive people to being socially discriminated against and to gain a sense of inter-generational continuity.

As many other studies have illustrated, what sparks an adopted person to search for information about origins and to seek contact with their birth family members is complex (Rozenburg and Groze, 1997; Howe and Feast, 2000; Muller and Perry, 2001b,). There may be a number of factors that influence an adopted person's motivation and decision to search and these may intertwine.

Whilst some adopted people do not seek family background information and/or establish contact with birth relatives, Brodzinsky *et al* argue that all adopted people will be curious at some stage in their lives about their origins and birth family. 'In our experience, all adoptees engage in the search process. It may not be a literal search, but it is a meaningful search nonetheless. It begins when the child first asks, "Why did it happen?", "Who are they?", "Where are they now?" These questions may be asked out loud, or they may constitute a more private form of searching – questions that are examined only in the solitude of self-reflection' (1992, p 79). This universal search, as Brodzinsky has said, 'begins during the early school years, prompted by the child's growing awareness of adoption issues'. For those who already have contact with birth family members, curiosity levels may differ by the mere fact that they may know the answers to such questions.

The study by Howe and Feast (2000) provides a useful comparison with the study sample in terms of curiosity about origins. We mapped in some of the relevant questions from this research. The study included a sample of 472 adopted male and female adults. Their adoptions took place in the UK before 1975 and they were mostly placed before 18 months. Most of the adopted people, both searchers (those who actively sought information and/or contact with birth relatives) and non-searchers (those who did not do so) lived with similar questions about why they were given up by their birth parents and whether they resembled their parents either physically or in personality.

Much has been written about the importance of the adopted person having a strong sense of identity: knowing who they are and where they come from. The psychological benefits for adopted people of knowing the facts about their origins and receiving background information about it have been well established (Triseliotis, 1973; Sorovsky *et al*, 1974). Sants (1964) found that adopted people described feelings of 'genealogical bewilderment' caused by a lack of biological connection. The knowledge and insight that have been gathered through the studies about what lies behind adopted people's motivation to search has been an important driving force behind the opening of previously closed adoption records. It has illustrated the importance of choice and enables adopted people to develop a more coherent biography that links the past, present and future.

Another area of interest is whether or not gender influences an adopted person's desire to know more about their origins and search for birth parents. Triseliotis' (1973) study of 70 adopted people found that there was an equal split between men and women but subsequent studies have reported that more women than men (2:1) show an interest in the search process (Gonyo and Watson, 1988; Pacheco and Eme, 1993; Howe and Feast, 2000). It has been suggested that women's desire to search may be triggered at times of marriage, pregnancy and childbirth.

Whilst eight women in this current study had been relinquished and therefore had limited information about their birth parents and the circumstances of the adoption, for 64 women (89% of those who took part in the study) this was not the case. They had been "abandoned/left to be found", although in a very few instances a note with the child's name or other information was also found.

"Abandonment to be found" is relatively rare in the UK. Between 1977 and 2010, a total of 197 babies were registered on the Abandoned Children's Register in England and Wales,[19] 27 of these babies having been abandoned during the previous ten years. Although such cases tend to attract media attention, there remains a dearth of research material on child abandonment (Browne *et al*, 2012) and studies that explore the lifelong impact of being an abandoned child and living without information about genetic inheritance and individual family background (Mullender *et al*, 2005). Mullender *et al*'s small qualitative study with ten adopted people specifically investigated the responses to being abandoned as babies. They report that the participants had a strong need to know about their origins and that they faced questions about lack of knowledge of origins in addition to the concerns of other adopted people. The women in this study therefore provide a unique insight into how they and their adoptive parents have managed this lack of basic information about their genetic origins and the impact they feel this has had on their lives.

Thoughts about birth family and accessing information

We learned in Chapter 5 that the women had a range of experiences in terms of the age at which they were told they were adopted, how

---

19 Neither Scotland or Northern Ireland maintain an abandoned children's register.

openly their adoption was discussed with them, and how much information was shared as they were growing up.

Some of the women told us that their adoptive parents had retained as much information as they could, along with any personal belongings they came to the UK with – the outfit worn for the journey, an identity bracelet, a birth certificate, a passport and reports from the orphanage. A small number of women reported that broaching questions about their adoption or items associated with this was difficult.

During the face-to-face interviews for the current study, we asked the women whether or not they thought about their birth families during childhood and whether this changed in adulthood. These responses were then coded into three categories.

Figure 9.1
Frequency of thinking about birth parents

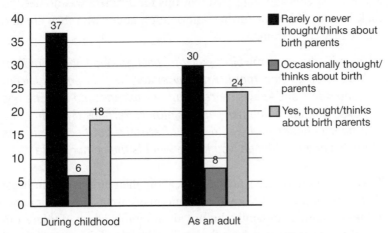

Coded responses for childhood, n = 61; adulthood, n = 62. Unclear/ambiguous responses not coded.

Although no direct comparative data are available, the proportion who rarely or never thought about their birth family in adulthood appears larger than would be predicted on the basis of other reported studies. The interview responses illustrated not only that the levels of curiosity varied within the group but that there was a range of explanations about why this was the case.

A closed door and impossible task

For those who rarely thought about birth parents, the most common explanation (given in a quarter of cases) was that the lack of options for finding further information meant there was "no point" in pursuing this. Sophie explained that, as an adult, she came to the view that:

Well, the thing is, when you are told from dot that you were left on the steps of the orphanage, it is very clear that you can't find somebody. So you don't even harbour those hopes.

Others put their lack of interest down to their closeness to their adoptive parents and suggested that this meant there was no need to look back or delve for further information about who they are and where they come from.

Even if I did know my birth parents' background I still would not have tried to find them. And my sister, who is adopted from Hong Kong, she knows more about her background and she has never wanted to find her parents either. Perhaps if I hadn't had a happy childhood, I would feel differently, but because it was such a good childhood, you know, what is the point? Maria

Interviews with women who did think about their birth family indicate that many of them felt close to their adoptive parents. In addition, not thinking about birth family did not always imply a lack of interest in learning about them or about their origins. Some of these women had visited Hong Kong or sought access to their orphanage records. One participant, who had put more time and energy than most into learning about her pre-adoption experiences, including tracing the policeman who had found her, explained why her birth family was not her central focus.

I suppose I have been so wound up either trying to deal with the

racism here or trying to fit in that I have never considered finding [my] birth family. I do say to people I have got more chance of winning the national lottery really, and that would probably have a bigger impact on my life right now. Katy

It is not unusual for adopted people to report that their adoption can be a source of curiosity for others and this group was no exception. Having to explain – sometimes to strangers – why they had not searched for information about their birth family could be frustrating.

I've said to people, well, because I've nothing to go on. They look at me like, oh yeah, she just isn't bothering, which isn't the case because I really don't think I've got anything to go on. If I was to go back there, I'd just be on a hiding to nothing. Grace

Comparison with those adopted people who have information and can search

Others compared their situation with UK-born adopted people. Some of the women were acutely aware that their situation was different but this was not always seen to be a negative.

I always have this thing about . . . when adopted people, foreign or just English, when they say, oh I don't feel complete because I don't know who my birth parents are . . . I don't feel that at all, I just think, oh well, feel lucky that you were adopted by people that wanted you. But no, I certainly don't have this idea that I'm incomplete because I don't know who they are . . . Lesley

At the reunion that we had with 23 girls and talking to all of them, except perhaps one, all of them had been back to Hong Kong to look for where they were left or abandoned or they wanted to look for the orphanage where they stayed. And I thought that was very interesting because they all wanted to find their roots and I just thought 'Oh well . . . roots? What are roots?' My roots are the family that bought me up and I have no desire to go back to Hong Kong to find my roots. Paula

One of the things that was good about not knowing was that I have got friends who are adopted and have always harked on about trying to find their parents and being in kind of constant angst over it. That has never been a possibility for me. The door was always closed on that. So I haven't had . . . Oh, maybe I am this, maybe I am that. I have never really developed or harboured any prospect of that. So no expectations, I suppose you could say. Alicia

Acceptance and coming to terms with the situation

Having no choice but to accept the fact that there was no information, some women said that it was more damaging to well-being to become preoccupied, they just had to accept the situation.

You just psyche yourself into thinking, I'm feeling so sorry for myself and depressed thinking I don't know who my parents are. You could get too psychologically worried about that. I just think I've been so lucky. Again it would be different if I knew I was a white adoptee and you knew there were all these records so that you could go back when you are 18 and you could get in touch with somebody and it worked out that they were lovely. There's a whole procedure you can carry that through, but because I knew there was never any chance, it's like you can't do anything about it. Marion

Imagining birth parents

Among those who had thought about their birth family more frequently, curiosity about physical resemblance or shared characteristics with birth family members was commonly reported. For some women, birth parents were less of a focus than wondering whether they had siblings. Others reported that they were less curious about their birth father but did wonder about their birth mother. Cathy gave a particularly full response:

I wonder what my birth mother is like, or would be like. Is she still around? Was she cold, warm? Was she nice? Does she have

other children? Why did she give me up? What was wrong with me? Because that is what you first think of, what is wrong with me? I have heard the other side of the coin, that there was a lot of poverty, baby girls were not particularly accepted, they wanted boys. Mothers just could not keep us, they had not got enough food. But that does not really detract from the first question you always ask: what was wrong with me? Do I have any brothers and sisters? But I kind of have to squash that a little bit because if I sat and pondered I think I would be really depressed.

A smaller proportion (six during childhood, eight during adulthood) described thinking about their birth families and their origins occasionally but that this was not usually a major preoccupation.

I do wonder, but it's not always in the forefront, it's there, at the back of my mind. I suppose in a sense it goes in this little box, it's got to be contained somewhere. Valerie

For Marion, the issue was not at the forefront of her mind although there were always reminders such as observing similarities that family members may share.

The only thing is when you look at photos they say, 'Oh, you've got their nose or you've got their eyes sort of thing or their bone structure,' and you sort of think, oh, I wonder what my mother would have looked like or I wonder what my father would have looked like?

Carol, when asked how much she thought about her birth parents, responded:

It sounds awful but I probably only think about my mother. I have never really wondered what my father was. Obviously I have got a father somewhere but it has always been that I wondered why she gave me up.

177

In some cases, thoughts about birth family only arose at particular times, for example, around the time their own children were born or when asked for a medical history. This experience of the triggers that provoke such thoughts is consistent with other studies of adopted people, who have not been abandoned (Howe and Feast, 2000).

I only really thought about it much more when I had my own baby. It's really quite extraordinary that I didn't really think about it, especially from my natural mother's point of view . . . Only in the sense of when I had [my daughter] I realised . . . what an enormous thing it is to have a child so to actually have to give it away . . . Occasionally, I might feel guilty that I haven't made more effort to find my natural parents. I probably have thought about it more as an older person but I never thought about it at all as a child. Angela

Tina not only thought about her birth mother following the birth of her child but also sadly when her daughter died. She recalled how she had probably experienced the same feelings that her birth mother had after she had given birth and parted with her.

There was a moment when I gave birth to my daughter, who was my first born, when I looked into her eyes and saw her, I was thinking, wow, maybe this is what I looked like when I was her age, so it was my first look really, and so that was a really profound moment for me. Then when she died, it made me think of how my mum must have felt when she had to give me up, so that was also another profound moment.

Some people thought about what it might be like if there was an opportunity to meet birth family members, as in the case of Jackie and Josephine who expressed concern that it might not be a fulfilling experience. They attributed this to the fact that they had lived very different lives from that of their birth parents, both culturally and also because of the language barrier. They were very aware that this would inevitably make communication extremely difficult.

The only thing that I really want to say if I could meet my birth mother is thank you for doing what you did but ultimately ... she would be a stranger to me, we would be strangers to each other ... it is a big can of worms, isn't it, to look in and walk down that road. What would I be looking for? What would she be looking for? What would we be expecting from each other? And I personally don't feel the need to go and look for my birth parents even if I could do it easily. I am still not sure if I feel the need. Maybe I will change in 20 years' time. Josephine

Sometimes I think how would I feel if I had someone in front of me who said 'This is your ...'? I think I could accept it, but I wouldn't suddenly have that total huge emotional warmth or bonding or anything, it would take some time to adjust to. Jackie

Accessing information from the adoption agency

Eleven women (16%) had contacted the adoption agency and or International Social Service (ISS) to request access to the information held in the records. This is a relatively low figure in comparison to UK-born adopted people, about whom it has been reported (Muller and Perry, 2001a) that about half would seek further information and/or try and locate birth family members at some point in their lives. One explanation could be that whilst there was no information about family background in the majority of cases, some of the women were not aware that there was information about where they were found and the amount of time they lived in the orphanage. Some also thought that as they had been adopted from overseas, no records would exist or it may be difficult to locate and gain access to them. These factors may well account for the reason why many of the women had not approached the adoption agency to access information.

As a result of being involved in the study and becoming aware that records relating to their adoptions existed, some women have subsequently decided to obtain access to this information and this figure is therefore likely to grow.

Making the decision to obtain more information

Making a decision to try to obtain further information about their adoptions was not taken lightly. The women who had thought of doing this considered the benefits and drawbacks. The following account illustrates this and sums up the thoughts of a lot of the women in the study regarding their reticence in trying to obtain information and/or in locating birth parents.

> *Part of me thinks well, if I did go down that route, and the likelihood is that I won't find anything or I still can't . . . how would that leave me? How would I be able to close that door again and continue with my life, because on some levels, from what I have observed both professionally and personally, once you open that door, you open it.*

Other women described themselves as content even to have a small amount of information.

> *I am happy with what information I have got. The pictures I have got, the experience I had. The fact that I took my adoptive mum over there, and that we met some of the Chinese girls . . .* Alison

Other women who made a decision to search for more information found that beginning the process only highlighted how little was known to them and how unlikely it was that they would be able to meet birth family members.

> *I had hoped to try and trace my family. I was able to take the record away with me and it doesn't say much – says very, very little . . . [age] nought to two. There's a hole and actually even though my [adoptive] parents tried to fill as much of that hole as possible, it's a hole. I would like to try and fill that hole as much as I can, but you know, how?* Miranda

The decision to seek information was not always driven by the adopted people themselves, as in some cases a parent or partner was particularly encouraging. Cathy's parents were very keen for her to have all the information they had relating to her adoption.

I had read some of the information but it was very, very difficult. Once I got the information, I just left it in an envelope until I was ready to read some of it, because emotionally I was not ready for it. Cathy

Erica, who had not been abandoned, told us that her parents were concerned about whether they had given her all the information available relating to the circumstances of her adoption and whether it would have been helpful for her to have more.

It was my decision [not to seek further information] and my choice and I don't think it was influenced by Mum and Dad. It was from me, to not want to explore ... because Mum's saying now, 'Well, is there anything more we could have done for you?' And I said no, because I think it was my choice. I don't think more information would have helped because more information wouldn't have made anything right. There was still a miserable set of circumstances and all the significant people around me died. I don't think you can make it more palatable than that.

Other women had considered seeking information but in many cases questioned whether such information would be helpful if it was unlikely to lead to a reunion with birth parents. Other specific reasons cited for not pursuing this option ranged from questioning whether they really wanted to uncover any information that may be out there in case it caused distress as well as not wanting to upset adoptive parents.

Making connections – returning to Hong Kong

Ten women reported that one or both of their adoptive parents had travelled to Hong Kong with them for a visit to see their country of origin. Three further sets of adoptive parents paid for their daughter to visit Hong Kong upon turning 18. One woman also recounted that her adoptive parents went without her to visit the orphanage where she grew up. The majority of these arrangements were seen as positive gestures, but there were rare exceptions where the adopted person expressed a lack of interest and told us 'it would just be like a holiday' or that such a trip was a fulfilment of their parents' own wishes rather than their own.

Those who travelled to Hong Kong as teenagers with their parents did not always find it the profound "homecoming" experience that others have described.

I don't understand the significance. I mean I was really quite switched off. My mother just said afterwards, 'You were just not interested one iota'. And I only wish I had been mature enough to appreciate and take it in. But I wasn't. I was a teenager. So that is the only time as a family we have been out to Hong Kong. We later went out for our honeymoon to Hong Kong. And again, I never even thought about going to see the home. Whether it was still there . . . and I wish I had. I was too full of other things.
Cathy

Some women reported that they planned to return to Hong Kong in the future, while others have decided that, since being involved in the study and meeting other adopted women participating in the study, they would like to visit. Rita had anticipated what the positive aspects of the trip she was arranging would mean for her.

I guess it would be nice to know where you come from with regards to people and the whole shebang and that is why this trip to Hong Kong is really important to me because then I will come full circle. I will see where I came from, and maybe just a back street, a cardboard box there that stands for what I was in. And then I shall just move on. But you like to know where you came from to see how far you have come.

Reasons for returning to Hong Kong

In total, 41 of the 68 women (60%) whom we interviewed had been back to Hong Kong at some point in their lives. Two more women were planning to visit after the interview had taken place and more recent contact with some participants indicates that this number is likely to grow. Of those who had visited, the main reasons cited were as follows:

- 19 women (46%) went for a holiday or plane stopover;
- eight women (20%) went back to Hong Kong with the encouragement of their adoptive parents;
- six women (15%) said they were primarily motivated by curiosity about their origins and went specifically to visit the orphanage or the place where they had been abandoned or to meet workers from ISS.
- four women (9.7%) to visit family or friends living there;
- four women (9.7%) went for work or studies;

Although only six women said their primary reason for visiting was curiosity about origins, 19 women (46% of those who visited) said they had made efforts to visit the orphanage, the place where they were abandoned or ISS offices whilst they were in Hong Kong. At least five women had been to Hong Kong on more than one occasion and tended to express increased interest in investigating their origins on the second or third visits:

I was in the fortunate position of actually travelling [to Hong Kong for work] and it made me think, I've got the opportunity to look into this a little bit more because I wondered if I could do more root tracing, so I contacted the International Social Service in, I think, London as well, and they helped me get the name from the ISS in Hong Kong. I communicated with a lady there called Jenny and she basically, over some time, did a lot of root tracing. She arranged for me to visit Chuk Yuen, the orphanage in Kowloon . . . where I spent the first year of my life. Helen

The impact of returning to Hong Kong

The 41 women who had returned to Hong Kong recounted a range of experiences. Some found that it was like a "homecoming" and felt a real connection, while others described is as a time of healing. However, others did not have this experience and felt no more allegiance to Hong Kong than to any other country they had visited. They described feeling a little uncomfortable or as if someone would "find them out" for not being from the country.

For Isobel, she found the return to Hong Kong a positive experience and felt it helped her to resolve earlier feelings about her adoption that had been raised during a turbulent period in early adulthood.

To actually be in Hong Kong seemed to confirm or it just made sense to me. Then we went actually to find the door number because we had the information of the number where I was abandoned . . . And when we went to the number and I found the doorstep, the door was green and it was similar to what I had seen in a dream. I remember some people walking by thinking we were mad, sort of, why are you standing there crying over this doorstep? So in that sense, it was a real healing time for me. It was just weird being in a country where everyone looked the same. I couldn't get over that . . . it was a really good time actually. Sad but good. Isobel

One participant, upon visiting Hong Kong for the second time, said:

I can remember sitting on the coach, the transit to get back to the airport when we were leaving, and I remember there were tears rolling down my face. Nobody actually saw because I hid them, because I didn't want to leave. If anybody had said to me at that point you can swap places, you don't have to . . . I would have stayed. Because at that point I realised I actually needed to spend more time just being in Hong Kong to just soak up the feeling. Katy

For some women, one of the positive aspects about returning to Hong Kong was that they did not stand out. They looked like everyone else and they liked being anonymous.

I mean that was the first time I was able to walk down Nathan Road and realise that I did not have my eyes cast down because I looked like every single person coming at me, and it was the white tourists that stuck out . . . And it is an extraordinary feeling to suddenly be able to think, actually, as long as I don't open my mouth nobody is going to know that I am not from Hong Kong. Victoria

It's weird, every time I've been back I've felt like I've come home. As soon as I get off the plane it feels like home – it's strange, really strange. But then of course I couldn't speak Cantonese and I believe it's probably still Cantonese there at the moment, so then the communication problem would come. Lynn

A number of women in the study have told us that they would really like to know more about their Chinese heritage and to know exactly where they come from. This was further discussed in Chapter 8. However, what was interesting is that, whilst some women's accounts describe "fitting in" because they looked like everyone else, others did not share this.

Georgina describes how she felt very different from other Chinese people in Hong Kong.

I've been brought up in such a westernised life really. I was taller than most Chinese people and obviously I can't speak their language so I did feel quite an outsider but going back the first time was very emotional, I didn't realise what element of me was still thinking that I was originally from there – I found that quite hard.

Others described having had mixed feelings about returning to Hong Kong as in the following cases.

No, it was peculiar because I didn't . . . I didn't feel one or the other. You know, I didn't feel I was Chinese either. Whereas some people might have felt at home again . . . Maybe it was the language barrier, I don't know. But no, I didn't feel 'This is my home, this is where I came from'. Eva

Maureen described feeling less of a "homecoming" than other people seemed to expect her to.

I felt quite comfortable in Hong Kong, I mean, could probably live in Hong Kong, I couldn't in Shanghai. Shanghai was very alien to me in culture whereas Hong Kong . . . and I don't know whether it's just because it's got lots of British-ness about it . . . felt more familiar.

Little or no desire to visit Hong Kong
Some women said that in adulthood they had no greater wish to visit Hong Kong than other countries. When Paula met other women adopted from Hong Kong, she found that others expressed a much stronger desire than her to make such a trip.

I have no desire to go back to Hong Kong to find my roots. I would like to go to Hong Kong. I would like to go to Singapore. I would like to go to Australia. I would like to go to the Maldives. I would like to go anywhere. Paula

Sophie was not alone in reporting that she had travelled widely but never specifically to Hong Kong.

And my mum always said, 'Well, you can go back to Hong Kong one day'. I never felt the need to. I have travelled quite extensively over the years and Hong Kong is one place – one day, I said to my husband recently, one day perhaps, we could go when we are on our way to New Zealand or something. Get a stopover. But no burning desire that I must go to Hong Kong and trace my roots. Sophie

Some of the women reported how their parents were very supportive and offered to pay the fare to Hong Kong, but in Florence's case she turned this down.

Mum did say when I was 18 would I like to go over to Hong Kong for my 18th birthday and I said no. I know someone of that age would love to go but I said no because it would not mean anything. It would be like a holiday. My parents had brought me up from day one and my mum and dad have always been open and they said, 'You know, would you like to look for your parents?' And I said, 'No, you are my mum and dad and everything'.

Celia told us that she did feel some "mild curiosity" about Hong Kong and the thought of visiting had crossed her mind and how she felt sad when Hong Kong was returned to China.

I am not sure whether it is directly to do with that but I know on the day when Hong Kong went back to China I sort of felt weepy ... because I have never taken any steps to try and go back. Occasionally I have felt mildly curious but not curious enough to actually go back. But I did feel like a sort of door has closed and that is it now. It is all kind of closed off to me. But obviously it isn't, it was just that moment of ... otherwise no.

Testing for factors associated with thinking about birth family

More than half of the women in the study described low levels of curiosity about their origins, birth parents and adoption, increasing only slightly in adulthood. This curiosity was also low when compared with samples of UK-born adopted people, and raises questions about what might explain this. Is it because the absence of information from an early age created a general belief that curiosity was better limited because the chances of obtaining any significant information were likely to be impossible? Unlike adopted people in the Howe and Feast study (2000), the opportunities to answer questions, such as 'where do I come from' and 'who do I look like' were not open to them.

We used the data collected in the questionnaire packs to test whether frequency of thinking about birth family in childhood or adulthood was linked to any of the following: age at which they were told about adoption; whether adoption was discussed openly within the family; whether they felt comfortable discussing adoption with their family; whether they felt their parents had shared all the information they had; and, looking back, how positively or negatively they viewed their adoption experience. We found no statistically significant associations. Although the sample size may make such differences difficult to detect, the women's responses suggest that the factors that influence a person's level of curiosity and their approach to managing this part of their life are complex and highly individualised. The question remains that if the women in our sample had not been abandoned and had had the same opportunity to gain to access information about their origins as the majority of UK-born adopted people in their generation, would their curiosity levels have been higher? Is the apparent lack of interest in origins by some of the women a natural suppression due to the fact that they were aware at a very young age that there was no information to be had? As referred to earlier, there is a dearth of information about the impact of abandonment on adopted people and how they are able to achieve a "complete" sense of identity without being able to link their past, present and future.

Conclusion

The information gathered for this chapter presents the views and experiences of a group of women who had little or no chance of tracing their birth parents or obtaining detailed information about their adoption. Many of their thoughts echo familiar themes voiced in other research, in compilations of adopted people's experiences, and in testimonies. The views of the women who were curious about their birth family ranged from wondering why they had been relinquished or abandoned to what it would be like if they were able to trace and meet their birth parents.

As noted earlier, these women differ from the majority of adopted people in the UK, for whom deciding whether to seek information and a reunion with birth family members is, at least potentially, a very real choice. The women in our research, even those who were relinquished, are unlikely to have had access to accurate and sufficient information to trace birth family members (because these records do not exist) or have only minimal information about their origins. People who know the circumstances that lead to separation from their birth family may need to find a way to manage and live with this knowledge. In contrast, those who do not have access to such information have to process a lack of knowledge about events that shaped their early experiences and subsequent lives. This difference may explain why more than half of the participants reported that they rarely or never think about their birth family. It does not necessarily mean a lack of curiosity about their origins.

Although we did not find strong associations between experiences in the adoptive home (such as openness in talking about adoption) and thinking about birth family, there are some clear strands to the women's narratives. For some, not thinking about the birth family was a deliberate strategy to deal with a lack of concrete facts. Metaphors, such as "a closed door", were used to illustrate this. For others, the birth family was not the focus of their reflections but they did wonder what their lives would have been like if they had remained in Hong Kong or sought information about the orphanages. Lack of information was not always seen as a negative. Some believed that this made it easier to cope by virtue of having to accept that there was no choice to be made and accommodating this fact within their lives. Attitudes towards these very personal issues were not formed in isolation; other people, from family members to strangers, expressed opinions that sometimes influenced the adopted person's thoughts, feelings and decisions. These could be benign or welcome but some were considered intrusive.

Reflecting on and managing feelings about origins is a consequence of individual circumstances and social contexts and may combine different perspectives that change over time. Of course it is not only adopted people who are interested in finding out about family background and origins; many people share this interest as reflected by the popularity of published memoirs, television programmes and websites about family ancestry.

One further point bears consideration. At the time of these interviews, only a small number of the women had met each other as adults. In recent years, a network of adopted people from Hong Kong – nearly all women – has started to develop and continues to expand. Although the study was not designed as an intervention, asking the participants to reflect on their origins and alerting them to the existence of this network has, in many cases, acted as a catalyst. Not only have a number of women subsequently sought access to their records, but more than two-thirds of the group have now met each other at various events. However, not all the women have chosen to participate in this reunion; some decided it was 'not a priority at the moment' and others felt that it would evoke feelings that they did not want to face. The findings in this chapter are a snapshot of these women's views at one point in their adult lives. The picture has already shifted and is likely to continue to do so as time goes by.

Summary

- Studies have revealed the complex reasons why some adopted people seek to access information and then search for birth relatives, whilst others apparently show no interest.
- Of the women who took part in the study, 89% were "abandoned/left to be found" and therefore had no knowledge about their birth families and the circumstances of their adoption.
- During both childhood and adulthood the largest group was made up of those who rarely or never thought about their birth parents.
- Many regarded their very early history as "a closed door" but this did not necessarily leave them feeling incomplete.
- Others wondered what it would be like to meet family members, about physical resemblance and shared characteristics.

- Thoughts about origins often lay dormant until triggered by an event, for example, having children.
- Visits to Hong Kong were common and reactions ranged from experiencing it as a "homecoming" to feeling no more allegiance to Hong Kong than to anywhere else.
- We tested whether frequency of thinking about birth family in childhood or adulthood was linked to any of the following: age of "telling" about adoption, whether adoption was discussed openly and comfortably with their family, whether all available information had been shared, and how they viewed their adoption experience. We found no significant associations.

10 Personal reflections on orphanage care, adoption experiences and messages for adopters

Introduction

We wanted to explore the women's views about having spent their early lives in an orphanage and the impact they thought this may have had on their lives as adults. This was of particular interest given the age of these women in comparison to participants in most other ex-orphanage adoption follow-up studies. At the time of participating in the study, the women were aged between 42 and 53 years; they were in their middle years, with experiences from childhood, adolescence and adulthood to reflect upon.

We also wanted to elicit the sample women's views about adoption, highlighting both positive as well as difficult experiences. Lastly, we asked them to tell us about their opinions on intercountry and transracial adoption and the messages they had for adoptive parents and other people in the adoption community. In addition to these three key areas, we also asked some general questions about their life satisfaction as a whole. We thought it necessary and important to have both quantitative and qualitative data for our analysis.

Effects of orphanage care

One of the key aims in this research study was to explore whether there were statistically significant links between the women's early experiences of orphanage care and adult psychosocial outcomes approximately 40 years later. In Chapter 4 we reported on our analysis of quantitative data taken from the ISS UK adoption files and the women's responses on a range of standardised scales. Here we report on the participants' own views of whether, looking back, starting life in an orphanage has had any effect on them in the long term. This question, as with others in this chapter, came towards the end of the interviews, when the women had already discussed their experiences in childhood, adolescence and as adults.

We categorised the responses as follows: 19 women said they thought starting life in an orphanage had no effect on their lives, 15 participants stated it had a positive effect (because of what followed), and 10 said it had a negative effect. Others did not know, either because they had not thought about it or because they could not comment on any consequences of experiences they could not remember. The quotes below begin to reveal the complex feelings that this question evoked.

As the majority of the women entered orphanage care after being found by strangers, such as a policeman or passerby, many of the responses to this question reflected this. As one woman explained, she was resigned to the fact that 'being abandoned was not wonderful', but to have a family rather than being brought up in an orphanage was a much better alternative.

Some stressed that these events had not defined their subsequent lives.

My life has been very positive – just because I have been separated and abandoned doesn't mean it has to have been an unhappy experience. Adoption or ethnicity should not be always used as a cause or problem. Paula

Among those who thought that orphanage care had "no effect" on their later lives, some put this down to having very little information and no memories about life in the orphanage. Others were more cautious, however, in reflecting on possible negative consequences, even if they felt it did not apply in their case. Erica, who viewed her adoption positively and told us of her close relationships with her adoptive parents, siblings and extended family members, expanded on this point.

I think by any measure it was a very poor start in life. Given the work I do and my knowledge of attachment theory, there was a

possibility that somebody in that position could end up with significant difficulties in making relationships. I was young, just eight months and probably quite developmentally delayed, so I kind of think that somehow it didn't affect me. I'm pretty well grounded and well balanced and have a positive attitude to life.

At the other end of the spectrum were women with more deterministic views. Some thought that the effects of their early experiences permeated their general worldview and had a noticeable impact across their lifespan. Patricia told us she felt she had been "hung up" on having been abandoned, which caused low self-esteem and had an effect on the decisions she made. Marion thought it had negatively affected her mental health and, in turn, this had created difficulties in raising her own children.

A recurring theme in the interviews was the idea that their start in life had led to a strong sense of self-reliance, as mentioned earlier in Chapter 6. There were mixed views on the consequences of this. Some credited it with helping them achieve academically or professionally or felt it made them better able to cope with life's challenges. By contrast, there was a group who described finding it difficult to trust or confide in others and considered this to be a lasting effect of very early events of which they had no memory.

I know that is where I get my independence from ... I have to acknowledge that my early childhood experiences have definitely influenced the way that I relate, my relationships, my level of trust of people. I guess the first person I rely on is myself. Katy

The opportunity to ask the women for their own views on the effects of orphanage care offered an alternative perspective to the assumptions underlying the research design. Some of these – such as personality characteristics and patterns of partnerships – will be explored in greater depth in future analysis.

Reflections on the adoption

In the questionnaire pack we asked the women some specific questions about how they felt about being placed for adoption and their reflections on their adoption experience. As Figure 10.1 shows, the majority of the women viewed their adoption "very positively" or "positively" with fewer than 10 who viewed it "negatively" or "very negatively". There was also a substantial group who expressed some ambivalence.

Figure 10.1
Looking back on your adoption, how would you view your experiences?

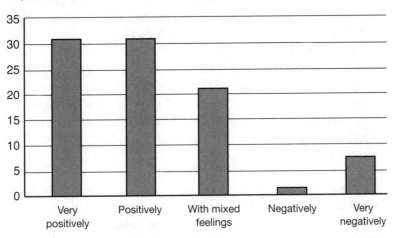

It was notable that many of the women's responses were shaped by comparisons with what their lives would have been like in Hong Kong. Most imagined they would have spent their childhoods in institutional care, and many thought life would have been marked by poverty and struggle or even that they would have ended up on the streets. This very low comparison point may lead to different conclusions from, for example, UK-born adopted people judging their adoptions against what life might have been like in their birth families or a different adoptive family. As one participant explained:

195

I live in a country where we are safe, free and prosperous - generally! My options in a children's home in Hong Kong would have been limited. Georgina

Many of the women touched on issues that were explored in Chapter 9, particularly feelings of "belonging" or a sense of connectedness to Hong Kong. Some told us that, although they loved their families and on balance were happy about being adopted, they still regretted the fact that they had to leave their country of origin. As one woman explained, there are many different aspects of being internationally adopted and unpicking these can be complex.

I love my mum and dad and my siblings so it is difficult to separate that and not feel as if I am being disloyal to them. I love them dearly. I guess somewhere along the line I wish I could have grown up within a Hong Kong culture, even if it wasn't with my birth family. Because what I have come to realise is I actually miss it. I don't know what I miss, but there is a loss there that I can't pinpoint. And whether or not that is a loss of heritage or a combination of everything, but there is a loss there that will now never be repaired ... the wrong word ... but which can't be overcome really.

The majority of those who viewed their adoption "very positively" or "positively", expanded their answers to explain why this was so. The most widely mentioned benefit was relationships with adoptive parents and in some cases siblings or other relatives: words such as "secure", "loving" and "happy" were used to describe family life. Others emphasised that even if there had been difficulties at times, they always knew their adoptive family would be there in "times of need". Josephine and Sandra were among those who were emphatic in expressing the advantages of being adopted.

Although being abandoned is not a good start, being adopted has been. I gained a family who have loved and supported me. There has always been love, honesty, compassion, empathy and open dialogue between all of us. My adoptive parents have always treated all the children exactly the same way so no one has felt any less or more than the other. My mother was very open-hearted and loved all her children, my father is a sweetheart. I am blessed. Josephine

Overall, I think having parents who really wanted kids and who definitely put a lot into bringing me and my sister up, and obviously some good things must have rubbed off because I am a pretty balanced kind of person, so I guess that comes from a stable, loving family and those sorts of things. So I am really lucky in that respect and all the opportunities that that has brought . . . you know, being hugely privileged really. Sandra

Like Sandra, many of the women felt that they would not be living in such comfortable circumstances if it had not been for their adoption and having been brought up by the family they joined. Some noted it was difficult to make comparisons because of having scant information about the circumstances they might have otherwise grown up in, but for others it was more clear-cut.

My parents gave me a safe and stable upbringing and I had a happy – albeit a little dull – childhood. I am certain to have fared better in this society/culture than as an unwanted/poverty-stricken child in Hong Kong. Lorraine

It was also common for participants to value the fact that they were given opportunities such as access to a good education. Such feelings were not always straightforward, however. Those who viewed their adoption with "mixed feelings" tended to refer to a range of gains and losses, for example, growing up in a family but still having a sense of "not belonging"; or having a strong sense of appreciation for the positive aspects of their lives coupled with longing to know how life might have turned out if they had not left Hong Kong.

For some, their feelings had fluctuated over time. This could work in both directions. Sometimes, challenging periods during adolescence or early adulthood gave way to more positive feelings, or changes such as having children themselves, which forced a reassessment of how they felt about earlier events. Alternatively, some women found that, as they grew older, being adopted became a more significant issue.

With the naivety of childhood, I was totally accepting. For early adulthood I very much still wanted to please and remained "loyal" to my parents. By my mid-thirties, I rejected much of their "hold" and attributed the ability to be able to do this act of detachment to being adopted. Angela

Others took a more pragmatic stance and professed that being adopted was not something they thought of often. This group was distinct from those with very positive feelings, however, as it did not necessarily imply that everything had been rosy.

I feel neutral about my adoption – it's just a fact of life. The issues I have faced have mainly been connected with race/ethnicity, and my mother favouring my older sister over the rest of us, including my brother who is her birth child. Celia

Around one in ten women viewed their adoption as a negative or a very negative experience. Although this proportion was relatively small, the impact on their lives should not be underestimated. We know that one of our participants, who recounted an unhappy childhood where she had felt unloved and not accepted by her family, was eventually received into care, which made her feel even more rejected.

Not surprisingly, the women who looked back on their adoption as being an unhappy event were mostly those who recalled a lack of acceptance, warmth and love during childhood. Some told us they felt they were an "outsider" in their family or that relationships were difficult, as one participant told us:

I had an abusive, bullying mother and think acquiring a child from overseas was more than she could cope with and she felt inadequate and insecure about her deficiency. Sophie

For some, the focus was more on the losses associated with leaving their country of origin and not knowing anything about their birth families. One participant told us that her adoption was a "disaster" and added 'I was denied part of who I really was – I lived, but at what ongoing cost?'

Some women who described an unhappy adoption experience reflected that this may have been because their parents and families had not been given enough preparation prior to and support after the adoption about the implications of adopting a child of a different ethnicity from overseas.

There seemed to be little planning or preparation for my parents to adopt a foreign child so they were never either aware or not able to offer any support with race-related problems which continue to date, for example, racial abuse. I seem to be the unwanted consequence of a hasty good deed. Hayley

The range of issues raised in response to this question highlight what adoption can mean for individuals. However, we also wanted to get a sense of to what extent adoption, whether described largely positively or otherwise, was seen as a dominant feature of these women's lives. Forty years on, had other experiences – partnerships, parenting, career success or setbacks, moving to other areas or even countries – come to be viewed as more important in shaping their current lives? Or were their experiences as very young children still the first thing to spring to mind when asked about major life events? We therefore asked the women to list first the most positive and then the most negative events in their lives since they had been adopted.

Meeting a boyfriend or partner or getting married was one of the most prominent themes, mentioned in 43 cases (60%), closely followed by having children (32 women; 44%) or in a few cases grand-children. Adoption and adoptive family life were noted in different forms: from a "good start in life" to relationships with parents, siblings or other relatives. For this largely well-educated group of women, gaining a degree or other academic achievements was cited by nearly half the participants, and a similar number referred to their employment history, either specific jobs or being happy with their career over the long term. The birth of siblings or attending significant family events such as weddings was mentioned by around one in five women, as was moving abroad or taking family holidays. Seven women specifically referred to making links with their country of origin – either having visited Hong Kong or having learned some Mandarin or Cantonese – including one who mentioned having sought access to her adoption records.

The negative experiences reported also focused on similar major life events, with deaths of parents and, in some cases, siblings or parents-in-law cited in about a third of cases. Divorce or breakdowns of significant relationships were mentioned by a quarter of the women, and severe health problems or periods of unemployment also featured prominently. Around half of those who viewed their adoption negatively, raised this again, with specific examples, such as continuing difficulties in relationships with adoptive family members, as constituting a major life event.

As we gave no pre-set categories in our questions, these were spontaneous responses; generally they confirmed the picture that had emerged in other data collected for this study. As time passes from the point of joining their adoptive families, other life events have taken place, which have prominence in the women's lives. Few studies have been in a position to investigate the weight to attach to childhood experience in relation to numerous subsequent life experiences and events. We found here evidence that reflection on adoption and what it means occurs across the lifespan, with a varying impact at different stages. This process can involve developing new perspectives at different points in time.

Views about transracial and transnational adoption

As well as focusing on their own personal experiences, we also asked the women about their views on intercountry adoption generally. In the questionnaire pack we included the question: 'How far would you agree with the view that adopting from another country is a good thing?' This was further explored in the face-to face interviews when participants shared what messages they would give to parents who have adopted children from overseas and what support they thought the children might need.

Figure 10.2
How far would you agree that adopting children from another country is a good thing?

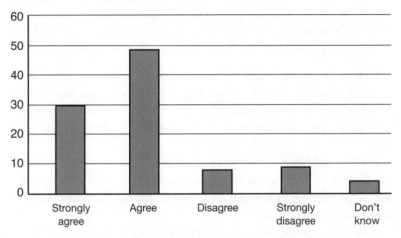

Five people did not respond; percentages are therefore from n = 67.

As the figures above show, the great majority of the women (78% of those who responded) on balance agreed that adopting children internationally was a positive step. Many included caveats that reflect wider debates about intercountry adoption as outlined in the introduction, for example, that it should only be considered where alternatives such as adoption by a local family are not available. Not all of the responses reflected the women's own histories; some supported the idea in principle despite their own difficult experiences and others expressed objections while stressing that international adoption had "worked" for them.

There were many reasons cited in support of children being adopted from overseas when local alternatives were unavailable, and although the women recognised the potential drawbacks, broadly speaking they considered that a child had the right and deserved to be brought up in a family where there was love, security and support. As with looking back on their own adoptions, the responses were often rooted in comparisons with life growing up in an orphanage. The following views were widely represented:

I think if a child has the opportunity to be brought up in a caring family unit, it doesn't matter where in the world that is. It gives a child a sense of self and belonging, providing the adoptive parents understand the culture they have come from. Maureen

I think it is preferable that children are adopted within their birth country, best for the child and the country. Where not possible, it is best to give a child a home than not. More often than not you're giving more than a home, it's a lifeline. Elaine

Some also added that intercountry adoption brought many other benefits for a child such as an opportunity to have 'a good start in life, full of fun and laughter, feeling wanted and special' (Jane) and to have a good education.

Ellen was unequivocal in her support:

Adopting children from other countries gives them hope, a future, happiness and the security of a family life. It could provide childless parents a way to have a family and give added richness and meaning to a family who already have their own natural children. Moreover, adoption could help a wider acceptance and understanding of people from other parts of the world.

Whilst the majority agreed with the policy of intercountry adoption, some felt there needed to be some conditions attached, with an emphasis on retaining some connection to the country of origin and on the lifelong implications of adoption.

I had a good experience and I think a loving family of whatever background is better than no family at all. I recognise, however, that not all children are as lucky. Adoptive parents should support a child's needs for his/her cultural identity and roots when it arises. Miranda

In principle, I believe your "family" is ultimately who you are brought up with, regardless of blood ties. If parents are able to allow the child to develop "naturally", the child should flourish – but the same also applies to blood children. The solution becomes more complex as an adult. Angela

Some told us that, whilst they understood the benefits that intercountry adoption can provide for the child, they thought it should be a last resort and that children should remain in their country of origin wherever possible. They acknowledged that intercountry adoption could provide a child with a loving family life and bring joy and happiness to the adoptive parents but were keen to point out that efforts should focus on ensuring that intercountry and transracial adoptions are not necessary in the first place.

On one level I don't agree with intercountry adoption. I really don't. I think there are other ways . . . all the arguments that people have for intercountry adoption can be counteracted quite simply. All the ones that say, well, we are giving these poor unfortunate children a chance in life. Well, yes . . . with the amount of money that it takes for you to adopt a child over to this country you could sponsor that child in their home country and allow them to grow up and economically put back into that country. By doing that you would give that country a chance of survival rather than withdraw their resources. Janice

A small minority disagreed with intercountry adoption as they felt that the losses outweighed the potential benefits and that it was wrong to uproot a child from their country of origin. One participant told us, 'Don't do it! Proceed with caution.' Some alluded to the high risks of the child feeling "alienated" as well as a lack of acceptance by others.

Although we have had the chance of a better life in the Western world, we have lost all our culture and language – we fit into neither a white society nor a Chinese society – we have lost our belonging (we have been denied). Cathy

Finally, some participants commented on high profile celebrities who have adopted from overseas; generally they were critical on the basis that it had become some sort of status symbol without due consideration of other possible issues.

It sounds hypocritical when it [adoption] worked so well for me, but I find it distasteful seeing celebrities collecting cute children from around the world. If a country experiences war or a natural disaster, I believe the way to help is to fund agriculture, clean water, schools, building and infrastructure. Not to remove the children – the potential workforce of the future. Erica

The range of views expressed by these women echoes recent and current debates on intercountry adoption practice and policy. It was striking how many of the issues described in Chapter 1 were present in the women's responses. On the one hand, there were concerns that intercountry adoption should be used only where the child cannot be raised by a family in their country of origin and about the potential losses involved in removing a child to another country. These were balanced against the many opportunities gained when a child can be brought up by a supportive and loving family rather than in orphanage care.

Another area we wanted to explore was the women's thoughts about the kind of advice and support they considered should be available for people who wanted to or had adopted a child from overseas. As a result of their own experiences of being transracially and transnationally adopted, the women had a range of suggestions, although some found this a difficult question to answer as they were aware that policy and practice have changed since the time they were placed with their families.

Others told us that the most important message is to be honest and open, particularly with information about their origins. They also said that it was crucial not just to think about the implications of inter-country adoption for a child but also for that child as an adolescent and adult. Some participants said that it was important for the adopters to allow the children to develop 'their own persona' but also to keep a close eye on them in case they were at the receiving end of race-based mistreatment.

Some responded that from personal experience it was crucial to ensure that children have access to networks where they will meet others adopted in similar circumstances. They stressed that children should not grow up feeling isolated and that more recent policy and practice should ensure that adopters are well-informed about such networks and their importance. Many were aware that such support groups have become much more common since the time they were adopted.

Conclusion

In this chapter we have described the women's reflections on two key markers in their life – experiencing orphanage care and intercountry adoption. The majority considered that their placement in a family for adoption was a positive event and gave them many opportunities that they otherwise would not have had if they had languished in care in the orphanage. However, not all of the sample felt this and a minority stressed the difficult and distressing consequences of being removed from their country of origin, which had repercussions for the rest of their lives.

Many considered that they had led a privileged life with plenty of opportunities to reach their full potential. They made it clear that it is important for children to be brought up in a loving secure family environment. However, they pointed out that both adoptive parents and the children should have access to information, advice and support and that this should continue over the long term. They emphasised the importance of children retaining links with their cultural origins to help minimise the likelihood of feeling isolated and different.

Summary

- The study women were asked to reflect on their lives from the vantage point of mid-life.
- Only 10% thought orphanage experience had had a negative effect on their lives.
- Only 10% viewed their adoption experience negatively; 20% had mixed feelings.
- A common experience was to regret separation from birth family and country of origin, but nevertheless to value being brought up in a secure, loving family with good life prospects.
- Although adoption was recognised as a key turning point, later life events contributed greatly to the review of their lives, especially partners, marriage, children, education and careers.
- The majority (78%) agreed that intercountry adoption was a good thing, but with many caveats about prioritising placement in the home country, adequate preparation of adopters, and the availability of support over the long term.

11 Adversity, adoption and afterwards – key findings and implications for policy and practice

In this final chapter we summarise the key findings of the study. The details that support our conclusions can be found in the preceding chapters. We then reflect on these findings to explore some of the related policy and practice implications. By necessity, these reflections and their implications are selective and limited by what it is reasonable to address, given the nature of the study.

History of the women and this research

The study has had a long history and much has been learned along the way with much still to comprehend. There are two strands to this history. The first is the history of the women themselves. As outlined in Chapter 1, our understanding from the ISS UK files is that the girls were probably born into circumstances of great stress, to parents who were part of the vast influx of refugees from mainland China into Hong Kong. It is likely that, as a result, they were living in circumstances where overcrowding, poverty and ill health were common and posed serious problems for many families. As a result, the babies who became the subjects of the study were mostly abandoned but in such a way that they were highly likely to be found quickly.

The care these babies received on entering the Hong Kong orphanages was, by the standards evidenced in many other countries, reasonable. But while it did not reflect the severe global deprivations of the Romanian or, indeed, orphanages in many other countries, it was still institutional care and, in that sense, sub-optimal to what we know very young children need for their development. It may indeed not have been untypical of many of the institutions that were in operation in the UK at that time (Robertson, 1971). Hodges and Tizard (1989a) note in their study of children in UK institutions that by age two, a child would have experienced, on average, 24 different carers and by age four, 50 carers. We do not know the precise figures for changes in carers over the course of a day or week for the girls in the Hong Kong institutions but it is likely to have been significant. Although some malnutrition was in evidence, routine medical care was available. Stimulation was possible at a low level but very much compromised by the inevitable absence of individualised, sensitive and responsive care, which is widely accepted as essential for the optimal development of children. To be adopted out of these sub-optimal environments into a country and families that were undoubtedly marked by opportunity, resources and individualised family care can be seen as acts of sensitivity, appropriateness and generosity.

The adoptive parents who took these children were in many cases motivated by the widespread media exposure of the conditions in Hong Kong during World Refugee Year in 1959. These were not intercountry adoptions marked by organised or specific acts of exploitation, injustice or betrayal that have blighted the reputation of adoption from overseas.

The second strand of this history is that of the research itself, although that history is more condensed. However, it is still a history that stretches back to the mid 2000s when the existence of the files of the 100 adopted children first became known to us. The files contained information in some detail of the circumstances of the adoptions at the point both before and shortly after the child was placed. Given that this was a complete group of internationally adopted children, now women in mid-life, this was an unmissable opportunity for research. However, there were still the requirements, which took some considerable time to address, of funding the study, designing it to ensure its worthiness and rigour, ensuring correct ethical standards were in place, and most important of all, tracing the women. It must have been something of a shock to be contacted by a representative of a group of stranger researchers who wanted to know what their lives had been like over 50 years or so. It was truly surprising that we were able to trace through public records 99 of the women and that 72 of them gave their consent to participating.

Science imposes its own strictures on what can be reliably known and that usually requires turning to *groups* of people and the various patterns that can be identified within a group or between groups. These patterns can be snapshots at a particular point in time or the ways that patterns change over time and what influences that change. Individual experience might easily get lost in those patterns although in this study, face-to-face interviews, often at some length, captured and allowed us to gain insight into these individual perspectives. The importance of designing a study using a methodology that is well established and accepted as rigorous by the scientific community cannot be underestimated. There are many views about what influences human development and what maximises the individual's satisfaction with, achievements of and sense of well-being about what has happened to them over their life course. The methodology we chose needed to be rigorous and informed by these ongoing debates about human development.

We accepted from the outset that people with similar early experiences could nevertheless have diverse outcomes and that a simple model of cause and effect in human development has already been largely discounted. We were mindful of the importance of acknowledging individual adaptability, vulnerability and resilience and their interaction with both stable and changing environmental factors such as the family, friendships, school and other life course events. We also knew that we could not specify all the independent variables – especially those to do with genetic inheritance and the circumstances of the girls prior to being taken into the orphanage. Finally, we had constantly to keep in mind that this was a female-only study and that generalisation to males was not warranted.

Brief summary of aims and methods

The study had three broad aims. The first was to document the lives of the women and to identify the variety of their personal stories. Much of the content of the face-to-face interviews was designed to record a systematic and detailed history covering significant life events.

The second aim was to conduct a systematic study in human

development by investigating the psychological status and circumstances of the group of women in relation to other suitable comparison groups of women. Such comparisons were essential for understanding whether differences could be identified when compared with women who had not experienced orphanage care and not been adopted. We were very fortunate in having access to a large volume of lifespan data from the UK National Child Development Study (NCDS) for this purpose (Ferri *et al*, 2003). This cohort, all born in one week in 1958 and therefore at about the same time as the BCAS women, contained women "typically" living in their birth families and a small group of non-abused or neglected women adopted as infants.

Finally, we wished to explore those factors that might influence who was doing well and who was doing poorly at the time of follow-up. Could developmental progress be explained by differences in the amount and type of exposure to orphanage care? If not, what might explain who had poorer outcomes and why?

We conducted a comprehensive assessment of psychosocial functioning at follow-up. By using standard measures and structured, coded interviews, we quantified the participants' responses, that is, we produced numerical data that could be analysed. We employed commonly used, reliable and relevant outcome measures enabling us to test for similarities and differences across groups and to check our predictions using relevant statistical techniques. Quantitative information was frequently examined alongside interview data, which allowed us to check for correspondences and differences and to explore the meaning of the responses in greater depth.

At the start of the study, we wanted to try to anticipate the outcomes for our sample before any data were collected. On the one hand, studies had consistently shown the deleterious effects of orphanage care, but adoption studies had shown remarkable remedial effects on developmental problems present at the time of placement. We predicted that our group, in carrying several risks, would show the effects of these over time. These risks were:

- lack of individual care in the orphanage over an important period of early development;

- lack of knowledge of family origins and the emotional impact of this;
- placement in an unrelated family where physical differences were transparent and were likely to present complex questions of identity and belonging.

As there is little theoretical work on adult outcomes that combines these three factors, it was not clear in which developmental domains any ill-effects might be manifest. As the members of the sample had atypical early relationships, we chose to direct special focus on their current relationship status, interpersonal difficulties and adult social and intimate relationships.

Features of the adoptive placements

We only know a little about the recruitment and selection of the adopters. By modern standards, a brief report was prepared on the couple by a social worker, which detailed their circumstances, and particularly their social and moral standing in the community. As with most adoption samples, the adopters were socially advantaged, with mostly stable lives and income and housing, and good education. One fact that distinguishes this group of adoptive parents from the majority of would-be adopters at that time is that most of them were already parents with experience of bringing up birth and, in some cases, other adopted children. Infertility was not a motivating factor for most of them. Almost all of the adoptive parents identified themselves as Christian, as might be expected as a result of the orientation of the adoption agency, and for some of them a "rescue" motive will have played a part. Some of the deeper psychological factors affecting the developmental needs of deprived children had not yet been recognised generally in family placement practice, and there was probably a general belief that, in adoption, "love was enough". Preparation for adoption for these families in the 1960s was very limited in comparison with current practice. For the most part, unless there were exceptional concerns, post-placement support was restricted to a few visits within the first year. These were largely, but not entirely, transracial placements, as 83 per cent of the girls were placed with adoptive families where both parents were ethnically white British.

Key findings

Growing up adopted – childhood and adolescence

On average, the girls were just under two years old when they arrived in their adoptive homes. The transition from an experience of impersonal group care to the intimacy of a family would have been a radical change, with no preparation, for them. The majority of the girls appeared to have been received into loving homes. When we examined the perceived adopter parenting style from the women's perspective, the majority said they felt loved by their adoptive mother and father. Even those who had experienced some difficulty in their relationships, particularly during adolescence, felt that their parents had been an important and valued source of support well into adulthood.

There were exceptions, with some adopters described as "cold" and, in a few cases, possibly harsh and rejecting. We attempted to identify variations in the quality of the adoptive parenting and questioned whether this was related to outcomes. We found that those women who recollected that, during childhood and adolescence, both parents demonstrated a notable lack of warmth, understanding and/or acceptance, had significantly worse adult psychological adjustment. We needed to be aware that we may have been hearing evidence of a more authoritarian or distant parenting style of the period and that these recollections of childhood may have been subject to a variety of omissions and distortions and not as valuable as contemporaneous measures. Nevertheless, the women's accounts from the detailed interviews, especially of rejecting and sometimes cruel behaviour, were extremely unpleasant to record and the specificity of the accounts suggested that the women had clear memories of upsetting and disturbing experiences.

Taunting and bullying were often reported in the school setting, with some of this focusing on visible physical difference. This was reported to be the cause of varying degrees of upset. During childhood, many women reported a feeling of "not fitting in" and suffered the discomfort of "being different". Because of the visible difference between the adopters and their child, acknowledging the children's adoptive status could not be avoided and most women – but not all – felt that their adoption was discussed openly with them.

The adoptive placements were largely stable, although five sets of adoptive parents separated and divorced during the women's childhood, and some women suffered a loss through parental death. Three of the children experienced what might now be judged as a disruption of the adoptive placement, although fuller information on the circumstances from both sides of the family would be needed to confirm this. The average age when the girls left home was 19 and most left for the usual reasons of training, employment and partnerships. A minority left as a result of relationship tensions in the family.

Given their early institutional experiences, it might have been predicted that cognitive impairments would have had a negative effect on educational progress. However, nearly all the women left school with some qualifications.

Policy and practice implications

Recruitment, preparation and selection of adoptive parents

The women's recollections of their adoptive parents' behaviour towards them during childhood offered many examples of sensitive, attentive and supportive parenting. The majority had continued to have positive relationships with their adoptive parents into adulthood. For a small, but not insignificant proportion of women, the treatment they reported when growing up went beyond the occasional expression of frustration to consistently rejecting or deliberately harsh punitive treatment by their adoptive parents. Predicting such behaviour by adopters is a highly challenging task for social workers and adoption agencies. The evidence from this study underlines the importance of the qualities required in adoptive parenting beyond that expected in "ordinary" parenting. Most of the adopters, who put themselves forward for generally altruistic reasons, went on to fulfill the requirements of this role in ways that appeared to be impressive.

In the modern context, prospective adopters are encouraged, indeed required in many countries, to explore the nature of adoption and its specific differences to creating a family with "born to" children. The decision to adopt usually marks a significant change in the lives of adopters, especially if they are dealing with the consequences of failed infertility treatments. Their life course generally will have provided them with both strengths and vulnerabilities that will enable and challenge them in this task. How they adjust to this new perspective in becoming parents and what their motivation is that informs this will be an important part of the preparation they undertake and the assessment undertaken by the adoption agency in exploring and supporting them in this transition. While there will be limits in what can be known and predicted before a child is placed, it is clearly important to identify significant risk factors before adopters are approved and children are placed.

As we have identified, there was a group of women in the study who recounted insensitive through to cruel parenting, and this has had significant consequences for them in the longer term. Identifying exactly what brought this about from this distance is difficult. Some of this may well have resulted from the adopters' motivation to adopt becoming frustrated by disappointment in the subsequent experience; this may have included hoping that it would be a solution to mental health problems such as depression, or because of unresolved issues of loss resulting from infertility, or an unsatisfactory marriage. Some of these issues may result from a lack of understanding of the needs the child and the fact that remedial or therapeutic forms of parenting may have been needed for children who had adapted emotionally and cognitively to early adversity in the institution.

Support during the childhood years for adoptive parents and adopted children

In those instances where there was harsh or cruel parenting, almost none of the women in the study had known to whom to turn during childhood to address such difficulties. The issues highlighted by this small group stress the importance of vigilance among all those who have contact with children, especially other family members or teachers and doctors, in becoming aware of possible signs of serious stress and potential ill-treatment in adoptive families.

Many of the women described how their views had changed as they grew older and thought more about their adoption. Some felt strongly that their parents should have been offered more support. Clearly adoption policy and practice since that time have been influenced by increasing understanding of the likely range of difficulties and stresses that adoptive families might face at different points in their life. The provision of evidence-based parenting advice has been a welcome advance, and as more is learned about the impact of early adversity on psychological and biological systems, the more this should help to shape effective support.

Experiences and outcomes in adulthood

How did the women compare with the NCDS sample groups?

When we compared the mental health and well-being measures with the adopted and non-adopted groups of women, we found no significant differences in mean scores. The proportions above the cut-offs on the key outcome measures (the GHQ and Malaise) were very close across the groups. Life satisfaction scores were almost identical. The proportions seeking help for various psychological problems (considered serious enough to consult a specialist) did not show differences. The proportions having sought professional help with emotional difficulties such as depression and anxiety were slightly lower (but non-significantly so) for the BCAS sample compared with the non-adopted and adopted groups. Only one participant had a serious psychiatric disorder.

The research interviewers made a rating after the end of each interview. Having listened in detail to the women's accounts of their lives and current circumstances, the interviewers assessed the women as having "superior" to "good" functioning on average across a range of areas for 87 per cent of the sample. This established clear evidence of positive outcomes.

Using four standardised measures of psychological well-being, we constructed a continuous outcome index. The two groups with the highest and lowest scores on the index were substantially different but with very few cases of extremely poor functioning. The interviews with those women at the poorer functioning end of the spectrum (15% of the sample) had more frequent contact with mental health services and greater instability in life histories. This included problems with partner choice and fraught social and intimate relationships. They were more likely to talk of a sense of abandonment or persistent sense of not belonging, but this was not universal. Of the 15 per cent rated as "better functioning", most described their adult home lives as relatively stable and happy. They recounted how they had recovered from challenges in life, such as relationship breakdowns or work-related stresses.

When we tested whether aspects of orphanage care were related to the outcome index, we found no significant relationships: for example, being placed at an older age in the adoptive home did not increase the risk of poorer outcome. We will continue to explore what other influences, or combination of influences, beyond that of orphanage care, determine differences in adult outcome.

It is striking that we found a lack of evidence of severe social difficulty as indicated by contact with the criminal justice system, long-term involvement with psychiatric care, or social services intervention in the care of children. Problems in functioning at this degree of severity might well be found in follow-up studies of children who were maltreated where they continued to experience adversity and disruption in their lives.

The strengths and limitations of the study have been noted in Chapter 4, but we stress again that these results apply to this particular ethnic group of internationally adopted women with a life course that began in the 1960s. Other studies would need to explore and develop our findings in relation to, for example, men, other ethnic groups, and adoptions from and in other circumstances.

Relationships with their adoptive parents
The majority of the women reported having good relationships with both adoptive parents throughout adulthood. The greatest difficulties were reported during adolescence with relationships under more strain. Such problems were not necessarily adoption related. Some women said they were not close to their adoptive parents, but only a very few had no continuing contact with one or other parent.

Relationships in adulthood
We were interested to know whether the women's early experiences of impersonal care in the orphanage might lead to a heightened risk of relationship difficulties in adulthood. For the majority of the women, they were currently married or in partnerships and the average length of relationship or marriage to date was nearly 18 years. The majority of their partners were white British. Two-thirds had become parents with an average of 2.1 children; four had adopted children. Further investigation of the extensive interview data may give a more complete picture of the nature and quality of social and intimate relationships.

Careers and employment
Following on from a prediction that cognitive abilities may have been affected by poor early care, how did the women fare in gaining post-secondary qualifications? As a group they were well qualified academically: more than a third had a Bachelor's degree and/or a post-graduate degree.

At follow-up, three-quarters of the women were in employment. A third were working or had worked in nursing or social care-related fields. Compared with the NCDS samples, they were more likely to have professional or academic careers, or to have held managerial or teaching positions. A number of the women had become notably successful in their careers.

Although many have travelled in their adult years, including visits to Hong Kong, and some have lived outside the UK, there was no evidence that as a group that they have spent their lives searching for a "lost homeland".

Although we did not intend to investigate the economic, social and environmental circumstances of the sample in any depth, it is worth noting that, over the period of these women's adult lives until follow-up (roughly the three decades – 1980s to 2011), it was largely a time of peace and increasing economic prosperity for most people in the UK. There was generally increasing freedom and opportunity in women's lives (although the playing field is still in need of levelling). Birth control and universal healthcare were available. Although there was a measure of social unrest and division and sporadic violence, it did not amount to ongoing political instability. Racial prejudice continues to be a reality in the UK, although, on the whole, hostility towards Chinese communities has perhaps been less visible than that targeted at some other minority groups. These factors are likely to have a bearing on the balance of stress and comfort that impinged on the life satisfaction and mental health of the women in our study.

Policy and practice implications

Evidence of the persistence of risk through middle childhood and adolescence has been important in this study. Our findings have led us to conclude that, followed up into mid-life, those with less severe risks do not seem to differ from the comparison groups. However, our findings also reinforce what had been learned in the Adoption Search and Reunion and Beyond Culture Camp studies: that adoption continues to have an impact across the lifespan and for some women that becomes more salient as time goes by and at certain periods in their lives.

What has been learned about accessing appropriate psychological services? Of those who had sought counselling or used other support services, many found them beneficial and in some cases described them as "life-saving". These women engaged in therapy to gain a better understanding of themselves and their life histories. We do not know enough in general about the accessibility and effectiveness of such services for internationally adopted adults, but from the women's accounts we were informed that support agencies need to be able to grasp the complexity of adults' needs where orphanage care and adoption are key historical features. On the other hand, it does not seem to have served the women's needs to put everything down solely to pre-adoption or post-adoption experiences. Furthermore, services need to be open to hearing about experiences of racism and discrimination and exploring strategies for dealing with them, although this is more than just an individual matter where it exists at an institutional level.

Physical health

The participants were asked to identify any long-standing physical conditions that affected them. One-third of the women reported some form of difficulty, with no single condition predominating. A range of health problems were reported but no longstanding physical problems for more than four per cent of participants. The incidence of diabetes, cardiovascular problems and epilepsy was very low. As a group, they did not appear to have elevated health risks.

The BCAS women's consumption of alcohol was much lower than either of the NCDS comparison groups, as was their rate of smoking, and they were more likely to take regular exercise. These positive lifestyle behaviours are likely to have an important impact on longer-term health outcomes.

Policy and practice implications

The findings from this study in relation to health are remarkable. It is known that children adopted internationally are likely to have exposure to malnutrition, exposure to drug and alcohol use by their mothers, risks from blood-borne viruses and from intestinal parasites and the lack of routine healthcare, such as screening and immunisation. The prevention of, screening for and treatment of these conditions must be a priority to maximise the developmental chances for internationally adopted children.

Questions about origins and access to information

We contrasted the experiences of these women, who generally lacked knowledge about their birth families, with people born and adopted in the UK, the majority of whom would have access to information about their origins. In the absence of such knowledge, we concentrated on how our participants thought about their birth families rather than their direct experiences of searching.

A small proportion of the women had already requested access to their adoption records and we know that a greater number decided to do so after participating in the study. Many women explained that a search for origins would prove fruitless and they regarded the door as closed. In contrast to most adopted people born in the UK, those without access to such information have to accept an absence of knowledge about their early lives. Those who were more curious about their origins said they wondered about their physical resemblance to their families and whether they had siblings. Some had used the limited information they had to build their own narrative about the circumstances surrounding their birth and early life.

Two-thirds of the women had been back to Hong Kong at some point in their lives and some had made efforts to visit the orphanage or place where they had been abandoned. We heard a range of responses about these experiences – from feeling it was like a "homecoming" to feeling little allegiance to Hong Kong as a homeland.

Policy and practice implications

The availability and openness of adoption records has been a major breakthrough in the UK for 30 plus years. It has become a fundamental right within a largely well-functioning system with appropriate age-related safeguards to access information and to establish links between birth family and adoptive family members. This is not to say that any of what happens subsequently is uncomplicated. In intercountry adoption that right is much more difficult to exercise and in many adoptions impossible because of legal barriers, poor records and national boundaries. This is clearly not in the best interests of those affected and the further development of international adoption should ensure that governments recognise this important right and put in place appropriate systems for ensuring that this right can be exercised.

Ethnic identifications

The women grew up in rural and urban areas across the UK – from central London to small farming communities. As the UK was not as multicultural in previous decades as it is today, those who grew up in urban areas did not necessarily have more contact with an ethnically diverse range of adults and peers than their rural counterparts; it depended on the specific area in which they lived and the people their families were in contact with.

We found that the women generally saw themselves as both British (via nationality and cultural socialisation) and Chinese (by genetic inheritance). However, there were those for whom this question did not lend itself to any straightforward classification. An important aspect of the study was to try to capture the extent of "connectedness to Chinese communities and culture" and the extent of "connectedness to UK society". A third of the sample was identified as having "some connection" to Chinese communities and/or culture. Active interest in Chinese communities and culture was not associated, as may have been predicted, with indicators of better mental health. What underlies an active interest may be complex. It may represent a drive to resolve certain identity issues, or it may be a way of dealing with other problems. Being connected with their local neighbourhoods was a positive feature involving regular socialising and feeling comfortable in public places and this was generalised to a broader sense of belonging in Britain. However, this does not discount the fact that, for some women, finding a way of "being Chinese" in relation to the rest of their life experiences has proved to be difficult.

The majority of the sample (72%) scored high on the scale of connectedness to UK society. Local socialising was common and virtually all felt comfortable in public places. The majority felt a sense of belonging in Britain and were comfortable being described as British Chinese.

When growing up, 44 per cent of participants felt comfortable with their Chinese appearance but this figure rose to 88 per cent when asked about their current feelings. Seventy-five per cent of participants reported times when they wished they looked less Chinese when growing up, but this had reduced to 19 per cent where they were currently struggling with this.

Most of the women had been on the receiving end of racism or prejudice in some form. This ranged from being called names (including as adults and not just in childhood) to experiencing discrimination at work. For some this included being physically attacked. Not all the perpetrators were white nor did all experiences take place in the UK.

Implications for policy and practice

As a consequence of their adoption, the women were dislocated from their country of origin and therefore from their ethnic, cultural, religious and language groups and identities. Many of the women grew up in isolation from Chinese communities in the UK and the challenges and difficulties this gave rise to have been identified and discussed. There has been an important shift from a view that this would have little significance on their subsequent development to one where it has come to be thought of as either having overriding significance or, as we have identified, that it has changing significance over time.

Sameness and difference in physical appearance, values, beliefs and traditions have enormous importance to human beings. The consequences of this are profound but, as we have found, not irrecoverably damaging, despite the arguments to the contrary. Adoption policy and practice have moved to a position where giving recognition to questions of sameness and difference, to belonging and not belonging, to feeling connected and disconnected, and the way that these weave themselves into an evolving identity, is very important. Adopters, in particular, have taken the lead in incorporating into family life lived experiences that support the recognition of what the child brings from their heritage. This has often led to the formation of self-help groups to support this. It is vital that children are given appropriate opportunity to explore, understand and celebrate their origins and address their experiences of difference. This must include in-family and community support when they experience discrimination and oppression.

As much as society has changed, the challenge of addressing these fundamental issues has not diminished, although a modern version of these issues needs to be openly acknowledged and developed to include a very strong emphasis on the child's experience and needs.

The women's reflections on international adoption

It was of great interest to know what the participants thought about the consequences of their early experiences. There was a spread of opinion on what effect they thought orphanage care had had on their lives, with a minority describing a negative effect of a lack of trust and problems with their identity. Some reflected on what might have happened to them had they not been adopted and one was even pleased to feel different. The vast majority said they felt positive about the fact that they had been internationally adopted after having been relinquished, although a small sub-group felt (and still feels) the effect to be very negative. Many said they were fortunate to have been brought up in a supportive and loving adoptive family and cited a good education and other life opportunities as benefits of being internationally adopted. They, like many adopted people, would have liked to have grown up with their birth parents, but given that circumstances did not permit this, decided on balance that their lives had turned out well. The frequency with which they reported thinking about their origins, as well as the feelings associated with this, varied greatly between and within individuals at different points in their lives. Those who reported negatively on their adoption lamented a lack of love, acceptance and understanding and felt a sense of isolation but some had gone on to build lives they valued despite these experiences.

Although many recognised the undoubted benefits of giving a child a good experience of family life rather than institutional care, many caveats were expressed: loss of culture and language and feelings of alienation, although the specifics of this very much depended on the quality of the adoptive home. Many were opposed to "celebrity adoptions" from institutions overseas.

For all the conflicting views about the merits of and arguments against intercountry adoption, we have been able to add to this debate by reporting on the views of a group of adopted women in mid-life. Three-quarters of the women agreed with the view that adopting children from another country is a good thing in specific circumstances, particularly when there is no viable alternative in the country of birth. Our study generally provides support for intercountry adoption in terms of a range of mid-life outcomes, but acknowledges that a minority of participants strongly disagree with international adoption and for many this has involved life-long struggles of varying degrees of intensity.

Policy and practice implications

The debates on the ethics and legality of intercountry adoption continue, as they have for many years. The profile of intercountry adoption is changing as countries develop their own domestic solutions for children relinquished or abandoned by their parent/s and where dominant belief systems – particularly the position of girls in society – have less sway. But there are still very large numbers of children at severe risk because of war, political and social unrest, famine and the absence of adequate practical and social support for families. Every finding from this study demonstrates the importance of and the significant advantages that flow from providing a family life for children in the context of reasonable practical, financial, educational, health and social support. That should not and indeed does not come as a surprise. But the development and resourcing of national policies that recognises the support families need in the care of their children still does figure high enough on the political agendas of many countries.

Conclusion

This study has been a remarkable experience with some very important findings. It clearly identifies the adaptability, resilience and strength of human beings when faced with significant early adversity. It attests to the importance of family life in providing nurture, care, stimulation and opportunity even when children have had a poor start in life. But it does not underestimate the challenge for those adopted and those who adopt. A child born to one family and raised by another will be faced by thoughts and feelings that directly arise from having a family tree with two sets of roots. These vary in significance and change over time. But for the group of women in this study, these thoughts and feelings have become incorporated in time into a picture of achievement, life satisfaction and positive outcomes, even though tinged with feelings of regret, a sense of loss and unanswered questions. It is our fervent wish that this should eventually be found to be so for all those children and adults whose life path is marked by adoption.

References

Adamson S., Cole B., Craig G., Hussain B., Smith L., Law I., Lau C., Chan C.-K. and Cheung T. (2009) *Hidden from Public View? Racism against the UK Chinese population*, Hull: The Monitoring Group and the University of Hull

Ansfield J. (1971) *The Adopted Child*, Illinois: Charles C. Thomas

Bagley C. and Young L. (1979) 'The identity, adjustment and achievement of transracially adopted children: a review and empirical report', in Verma G. and Bagley C. (eds) *Race, Education and Identity*, London: MacMillan, pp 192–219

Bagley C. and Young L. (1980) 'The long-term adjustment and identity of a sample of inter-country adopted children', *International Social Work*, 23:3, pp 16–22

Bagley C., Young L. and Scully A. (1996/2000) 'Adopted girls from Hong Kong in Britain: a twenty year follow up of adjustment and social identity', in Bagley C., Young L. and Scully A. (eds) *International and Transracial Adoptions: A mental health perspective*, Aldershot: Ashgate

Barker D. (2003) 'The developmental origins of adult disease', *European Journal of Epidemiology*, 18:8, pp 733–736

Barker D. J. (1995) 'Foetal origins of coronary heart disease', *British Medical Journal*, 311, pp 171–174

Barker D. J. P., Eriksson J. G., Forsen T. and Osmond C. (2002) 'Foetal origins of adult disease: strength of effects and biological basis', *International Journal of Epidemiology*, 31:6, pp 1235–1239

Barker D. J., Osmond C., Kajantie E. and Eriksson J. G. (2009) 'Growth and chronic disease: findings in the Helsinki birth cohort', *Annals of Human Biology*, 36:5, pp 445–458

Bifulco A., Bernazzani O., Moran P. M. and Ball C. (2000) 'Lifetime stressors and recurrent depression: preliminary findings of the Adult Life Phase Interview (ALPHI)', *Social Psychiatry and Psychiatric Epidemiology*, 35:6, pp 264–275

Bifulco A., Bernazzani O., Moran P. M. and Jacobs C. (2005) 'Childhood experience of care and abuse questionnaire (CECA.Q) validation in a community series', *British Journal of Clinical Psychology*, 44, pp 563–581

Bifulco A., Mahon J., Kwon J. H., Moran P. M. and Jacobs C. (2003) 'The Vulnerable Attachment Style Questionnaire (VASQ): an interview-based measure of attachment styles that predict depressive disorder', *Psychological Medicine*, 33:6, pp 1099–1110

Bimmel N., Juffer F., van IJzendoorn M. H. and Bakermans-Kranenburg M. J. (2003) 'Problem behavior of internationally adopted adolescents: a review and meta-analysis', *Harvard Review of Psychiatry*, 11, pp 64–77

Bowlby J. (1951) *Maternal Care and Mental Health*, Geneva: World Health Organization

Bowlby J. (1969) *Attachment and Loss*, London: Hogarth Press

Brodzinsky D. M. (2005) 'Reconceptualising openness in adoption: implications for theory, research and practice', in Brodzinsky D. M. and Palacios J. (eds) *Psychological Issues in Adoption: Research and practice*, Westport, CT: Praeger

Brodzinsky D. M., Schechter M. D. and Marantz Henig R. (1992) *Being Adopted: The lifelong search for self*, New York, NY: Anchor Books

Brooks D. and Barth R. (1999) 'Adult transracial and inracial adoptees: effects of race, gender, adoptive family structure and placement history on adjustment outcomes', *American Journal of Orthopsychiatry*, 69:1, pp 87–99

Browne K. D., Chou S., Whitfield K., naut M., Daniunaite I., Herczog M., Keller-Hamela M., Leth I., Matej V., Neagu M., Shalapatova I. and Zurovcova H. (2012) *Child Abandonment and its Prevention in Europe*, Nottingham: University of Nottingham

Castle H., Knight E. and Watters C. (2011) 'Ethnic identity as a protective factor for looked after and adopted children from ethnic minority groups: a critical review of the literature', *Adoption Quarterly*, 14, pp 305–325

Cederblad M., Hook B., Irhammar M. and Mercke A. (1999) 'Mental health in international adoptees as teenagers and young adults: an epidemiological study', *Journal of Child Psychology & Psychiatry & Allied Disciplines*, 40, pp 1239–1248

Central Advisory Council for Education (1967) *The Plowden Report (1967) Children and their Primary Schools. Part Two: The growth of the child*, London: Her Majesty's Stationery Office

Chisholm K. (1998) 'A three year follow-up of attachment and indiscriminate friendliness in children adopted from Romanian orphanages', *Child Development*, 69:4, pp 1092–1106

Chisholm K., Carter M., Ames E. and Morison S. (1995) 'Attachment security and indisciminately friendly behaviour in children adopted from Romanian orphanages', *Development and Psychopathology*, 7:2, pp 283–294

Collishaw S., Pickles A., Messer J., Rutter M., Shearer C. and Maughan B. (2007) 'Resilience to adult psychopathology following childhood maltreatment: evidence from a community sample', *Child Abuse and Neglect*, 31, pp 211–229

Dai Z. C. and Qi G. M. (1997) *Viral Hepatitis in China: Seroepidemiological survey in Chinese population (Part one)*, Beijing: Beijing Science and Technology Press, pp 39–58

Elliot J. and Vaitilingam R. (2008) *Now We are 50: Key findings from the National Child Development Study*, London: The Centre for Longitudinal Studies, Institute of Education, University of London

Endicott J., Spitzer R. L., Fleiss J. L. and Cohen J. (1976) 'The Global Assessment Scale; a procedure for measuring overall severity of psychiatric disturbance', *Archives of General Psychiatry*, 33, pp 766–771

Feigelman W. (2000) 'Adjustments of transracially and inracially adopted young adults', *Child and Adolescent Social Work Journal*, 17, pp 165–183

Ferri E., Bynner J. M. and Wadsworth M. (2003) *Changing Britain, Changing Lives: Three generations at the turn of the century*, London: Institute of Education, University of London

Frejka T., Jones G. W. and Sardon J. P. (2010) 'East Asian childbearing patterns and policy developments', *Population and Development Review*, 36:3, pp 579–606

Freundlich M. and Lieberthal J. K. (2000) *The Gathering of the First Generation of Adult Korean Adoptees: Adoptees' perceptions of international adoption*, available at: www.adoptioninstitute.org/, accessed 27 March 2012

Friedlander M. L., Larney L. C., Skau M., Hotaling M., Cutting M. L. and Schwam M. (2000) 'Bicultural identification: experiences of internationally adopted children and their parents', *Journal of Counselling Psychology*, 47, pp 187–198

Gatrell P. (2011) *Free World? The Campaign to save the world's refugees*, 1956–1963, Cambridge: Cambridge University Press

Gill O. and Jackson B. (1983) *Adoption and Race: Black, Asian and mixed-race children in white families*, London: Batsford Academic and Educational Ltd

Goedde H. W., Benkmann H. G., Kriese L., Bogdanski P., Agarwal D. P., Ruofu D., Liangzhong C., Meiying C., Yida Y., Jiujin X., Shizhe L. and Yongfa W. (1984) 'Aldehyde dehydrogenase isozyme deficiency and alcohol sensitivity in four different Chinese populations', *Hum Hered* 34, pp 183–186

Goldberg D., McDowell I. and Newell C. (1996) *General Health Questionnaire [GHQ], Measuring health: A guide to rating scales and questionnaires* (2nd edition), New York, NY: Oxford University Press

Gonyo B. and Watson K. W. (1988) 'Searching in adoption', *Public Welfare*, Winter, pp 14–22

Gunnar M. and van Dulmen M. and the International Adoption Project Team (2007) 'Behaviour problems in post-institutionalised internationally adopted children', *Development and Psychopathology*, 19, pp 129–148

Gunnar M. R., Bruce J. and Grotevant H. D. (2000) 'International adoption of institutionally reared children: research and policy', *Development and Psychopathology*, 12:4, pp 677–693

Hardt J. and Rutter M. (2004) 'Validity of adult retrospective reports of adverse childhood experiences: review of the evidence', *Journal of Child Psychology and Psychiatry*, 45, pp 260–73

Hawkes D. and Plewis I. (2006) 'Modelling non-response in the National Child Development Study', *Journal of the Royal Statistical Society*, 169:3, pp 479–491

Hjern A., Lindblad F. and Vinnerljung B. (2002) 'Suicide, psychiatric illness, and social maladjustment in intercountry adoptees in Sweden: a cohort study', *The Lancet*, 360: 9331, pp 443–448

Hodges J. and Tizard B. (1989a) 'IQ and behavioural adjustment of ex-institutional adolescents', *Journal of Child Psychology and Psychiatry*, 30:1, pp 53–75

Hodges J. and Tizard B. (1989b) 'Social and family relationships of ex-institutional adolescents', *Journal of Child Psychology and Psychiatry*, 30:1, pp 77–97

Hong Kong Council of Social Service (1960) *Newsletter, September*, Hong Kong: Council of Social Service

Hong Kong Council of Social Service (1961) *Working Together Newsletter no. 11*, Hong Kong: Council of Social Service

Hong Kong Social Welfare Department (1962) *Quarterly Report for April–June 1962*, Hong Kong: Social Welfare Department

Howe D. and Feast J. (2000) *Adoption, Search and Reunion: The long-term experience of adopted adults*, London: The Children's Society

Huang C., Li Z., Wang M. and Martorelli R. (2010) 'Early life exposure to the 1959–1961 Chinese famine has long-term health consequences', *Journal of Nutrition*, 140, pp 1874–1878

Hudson D. B. (1959) *Modern Parenthood: Keeping your child healthy and happy*, London: Pearson

Hutchin K. C. and 'A Family Doctor' (1968) *How not to Kill your Children*, London: Allen and Unwin

International Social Service (1958) *Memorandum 24/07/58*, Hong Kong: ISS

International Social Service Hong Kong (1961) *Newsletter*, April 1961, No 1, Hong Kong: ISS

International Social Service New York (1958) *Report March 1958*, New York, NY: ISS

Jackson B. (1976) *Family Experiences of Inter-Racial Adoption*, London: Association of British Adoption and Fostering Agencies

Jia J. (2008) 'Hepatitis B in China: from guideline to practice', *Virologica Sinica*, 23:2, pp 152–155

Juffer F. and van IJzendoorn M. H. (2005) 'Adoptees do not lack self-esteem: a meta-analysis of studies on self-esteem of transracial, international, and domestic adoptees', *Psychological Bulletin*, 133:6, pp 1067–1083

Keating J. (2009) *A Child for Keeps: The history of adoption in England, 1918–45*, Basingstoke: Palgrave Macmillan

Kim D. S. (1977) 'How they fared in American homes: A follow-up study of adopted Korean children in the United States', *Children Today*, 6, pp 2–6

Kirton (2000) *'Race', Ethnicity and Adoption*, 'Race', health and social care series, Buckingham: Open University Press

Kornitzer M. (1976) *Adoption*, London: Putnam

Lau Y. L., Chan L. C., Chan Y. Y., Ha S. Y., Yeung C. Y., Waye J. S. and Chui D. H. (1997) 'Prevalence and genotypes of alpha- and beta-thalassemia carriers in Hong Kong: implications for population screening', *New England Journal of Medicine*, 336:18, pp 1298–301

Laub J. H. and Sampson R. J. (2003) *Shared Beginnings, Divergent Lives: Delinquent boys to age 70*, Cambridge: Harvard University Press, Chapters 6–10

Lee M. M. C., Change K. S. F. and Chan M. M. C. (1963) 'Sexual maturation of Chinese girls in Hong Kong', *Paediatrics*, 32, pp 389–398

Lee R. M. (2003) 'The transracial adoption paradox: history, research and counselling implications of cultural socialization', *The Counselling Psychologist*, 31:6, pp 711–744

Li H., Ji C. Y., Zong X. N. and Zhang Y. Q. (2009) 'Height and weight standardized growth charts for Chinese children and adolescents aged 0 to 18 years', *China Pediatrics Journal*, 47:7, pp 487–92

Liang X. F., Chen Y. S., Wang X. J., He X., Chen L. J. and Wang J. (2005) 'A study on the sero-epidemiology of hepatitis B in Chinese population aged over 3 years old: the report from Chinese Center for Disease Control and Prevention', *Chinese Journal of Epidemiology*, 26, pp 655–658

Lindblad F., Hjern A. and Vinnerljung B. (2003) 'Intercountry adopted children as young adults', *American Journal of Orthopsychiatry*, 73, pp 190–202

Lindt A. (November 1959) *United Nations High Commissioner for Refugees Statement to the Third Committee of the United Nations General Assembly* (location unknown)

Logan N. S., Davies L. N., Mallen E. A.and Gilmartin B. (2005) 'Ametropia and ocular biometry in a UK university student population', *Optometry and Vision Science*, 82:4, pp 261–6

Lovelock K. (2000) 'Intercountry adoption as a migratory practice: a comparative analysis of intercountry adoption and immigration policy and practice in the United States, Canada and New Zealand in the post WWII period', *International Migration Review*, 34:3, pp 919–920

Mark C. (2007) 'The "problem of people": British colonials, cold war powers and the Chinese refugees in Hong Kong 1949–1962', *Modern Asian Studies*, 41:6, pp 1145–1181

Mason K. and Selman P. (1997) 'Birth parents' experiences of contested adoptions', *Adoption & Fostering*, 21:1, pp 21–28

McRoy R. G., Zurcher L. A., Lauderdale M. L. and Anderson R. N. (1982) 'Self-esteem and racial identity in transracial and inracial adoptees', *Social Work*, 27, pp 522–526

Miller L. (2005) *The Handbook of International Adoption Medicine*, New York, NY: Oxford University Press

Modood T. and Berthoud R. (1997) *Ethnic Minorities in Britain, The Fourth National Survey of Ethnic Minorities*, London: Policy Studies Institute

Mullender A., Pavolivic A. and Staples V. (2005) 'I have no beginning and no end: the experience of being a foundling', *Adoption & Fostering*, 29:2, pp 53–65

Muller U. and Perry B. (2001a) 'Adopted persons' search for and contact with their birth parents I', *Adoption Quarterly*, 4, pp 5–37

Muller U. and Perry B. (2001b) 'Adopted persons' search for and contact with their birth parents II: adoptee-birth parent contact', *Adoption Quarterly*, 4:3, pp 39–73

Murch M., Lowe N., Borkowski M., Copner R. and Grew K. (1993) *Pathways to Adoption*, London: HMSO

O'Connor T. G., Rutter M. and Beckett C. (2000) 'The effects of global severe privation on cognitive competence: extension and longitudinal follow-up', *Child Development*, 71, pp 376–390

Office for National Statistics (2005) *Focus on Ethnicity and Identity*, Colchester: UK Data Archive

Pacheco F. and Eme R. (1993) 'An outcome study of the reunion between adoptees and biological parents', *Child Welfare: Journal of Policy, Practice, and Program*, 72:1, Jan-Feb, pp 53–64

Painter R. C., de Rooij S. R., Bossuyt P. M. M., Simmers T. A., Osmond C., Barker D. J. P., Bleker O. P. and Roseboom T. J. (2006) 'Early onset of coronary heart disease after prenatal exposure to the Dutch famine', *American Journal of Clinical Nutrition*, 84:2, pp 322–7

Parker G., Tupling H. and Brown L. (1979) 'A parental bonding instrument', *British Journal of Medical Psychology*, 52, pp 1–10

Perry J., Sigal J., Boucher S., Paré N., Ouimet M. C., Normand J. and Henry M. (2005) 'Personal strengths and traumatic experiences among institutionalized children given up at birth (les enfants de duplessis-duplessis' children): II: adaptation in late adulthood', *Journal of Nervous and Mental Disease*, 193:12, pp 783–789

Portanti M. and Whitworth S. (2010) 'Lifelong childlessness in England and Wales: evidence from the ONS Longitudinal Study', *Longitudinal and Life Course Studies*, 1:2, pp 155–169

Quinton D. and Rutter M. (1988) *Parenting Breakdown: The making and breaking of intergenerational links*, Aldershot: Avebury Gower Publishing

Raynor L. (1970) *Adoption of Non-White Children: The experience of a British adoption project*, London: Allen & Unwin

Rich-Edwards J. W., Kleinman K., Michels K. B., Stamfer M. J., Manson J. E. and Rexrode K. M. (2004) 'Longitudinal study of birth weight and adult body mass index in predicting risk of coronary heart disease and stroke in women', *British Medical Journal*, 330, pp 1115–8

Robertson J. (1971) 'Young children in brief separation: a fresh look', *The Psychoanalytical Study of the Child*, 26, pp 264–315

Robinson L. (2000) 'Racial identity attitudes and self-esteem of Black adolescents in residential care: an exploratory study', *British Journal of Social Work*, 30:1, pp 3–24

Rosenberg M. (1965) *Society and the Adolescent Self-Image*, Princeton, NJ: Princeton University Press

Rozenburg K. F. and Groze V. (1997) 'The impact of secrecy and denial in adoption: practice and treatment issues', *Families in Society*, 78:5, pp 522–30

Rubin D. C. and Schulkind M. (1997) 'The distribution of autobiographical memories across the lifespan', *Memory & Cognition*, 25:6, pp 859–866

Rule G. (2006) *Recruiting Black and Minority Ethnic Adopters and Foster Carers*, London: BAAF

Rushton A. and Minnis H. (1997) 'Annotation: transracial family placements', *Journal of Child Psychology & Psychiatry & Allied Disciplines*, 38, pp 147–159

Rutter M. (2012) 'Resilience as a dynamic concept', *Development and Psychopathology*, 24:2, pp 335–44

Rutter M. and the English and Romanian Adoptees (ERA) Study Team (1998) 'Developmental catch-up, and deficit, following adoption after severe global early deprivation', *Journal of Child Psychology and Psychiatry*, 39:4, pp 465–476

Rutter M., Sonuga-Barke E., Beckett C., Castle J., Kreppner J., Kumsta R., Schlotz W., Stevens S. and Bell C. (2010) 'Deprivation-specific psychological patterns: effects of institutional deprivation', *Monographs of the Society for Research in Child Development*, 75:1, pp 1–252

Rutter M., Tizard J. and Whitmore K. (1970) *Education, Health and Behaviour*, London: Longmans

Ryburn M. (1992) 'Contested adoption proceedings', *Adoption & Fostering*, 16:4, pp 29–38

Sachdev P. (1989) *Unlocking the Adoption Files*, Toronto: Lexington Books

Sants H. J. (1964) 'Genealogical bewilderment in children with substitute parents', *British Journal of Medical Psychology*, 37, pp 133–141

Sigal J., Perry C., Rossignol M. and Ouimet M. (2003) 'Unwanted infants: psychological and physical consequences of inadequate orphanage care 50 years later', *American Journal of Orthopsychiatry*, 73:1, pp 3–12

Simmonds J. (2012) 'Adoption: from the preservation of the moral order to the needs of the child', in Davies M. (ed) *Social Work with Children and Families*, Basingstoke: Palgrave Macmillan

Simon R. J. and Altstein H. (2000) *Adoption Across Borders: Serving the children in transracial and intercountry adoptions*, Lanham: Rowman & Littlefield

Sorovsky A., Baran A. and Pannor R. (1974) 'The reunion of adoptees and birth relatives', *Journal of Youth and Adolescence*, 3, pp 195–206

Spock B. (1969) *Baby and Child Care*, London: The Bodley Head

Sroufe L. A., Egeland B., Carlson E. and Collins W. A. (2005) *The Development of the Person: The Minnesota study of risk and adaptation from birth to adulthood*, New York, NY: Guilford Press

Standing Conference of Societies Registered for Adoption (1950) *What should we tell our Adopted Child?*, London: Standing Conference of Societies Registered for Adoption

Storsbergen H., Juffer F., Van Son M. J. M. and Hart H. (2010) 'Internationally adopted adults who did not suffer severe early deprivation: the role of appraisal of adoption', *Children and Youth Services Review*, 32, pp 191–197

Syddall H. E., Sayer A. A., Dennison E. M., Martin H. J., Barker D. J. and Cooper C. (2005a) 'Cohort profile: the Hertfordshire Cohort Study', *International Journal of Epidemiology*, 34, pp 1234–1242

Syddall H. E., Sayer A. A., Simmonds S. J., Osmond C., Cox V., Dennison E. M., Barker D. J. and Cooper C. (2005b) 'Birth weight, infant weight gain, and cause-specific mortality: the Hertfordshire Cohort Study', *American Journal of Epidemiology*, 161, pp 1074–1080

Tan T. X. and Jordan-Arthur B. (2012) 'Adopted Chinese girls come of age: feelings about adoption, ethnic identity, academic functioning, and global self-esteem', *Children and Youth Services Review*, 34:8, pp 1500–1508

Tessler R. C., Gamache G. and Liu L. (1999) *West Meets East: Americans adopt Chinese children*, Westport, CT: Bergin & Garvey

Tieman W., van der Ende J. and Verhulst F. C. (2005) 'Psychiatric disorders in young adult intercountry adoptees: an epidemiological study', *American Journal of Psychiatry*, 162:3, pp 592–598

Tizard B. and Hodges J. (1978) 'The effect of institutional rearing on the development of eight-year-old children', *Journal of Child Psychology and Psychiatry and Allied Disciplines*, 19, pp 99–118

Triseliotis J. (1973) *In Search of Origins: The experiences of adopted people*, London: Routledge and Kegan Paul

Triseliotis J., Feast J. and Kyle F. (2005) *The Adoption Triangle Revisited: A study of Adoption, search and reunion experiences*, London: BAAF

United Nations (1960) *Report of Leysin Seminar on Inter-Country Adoption*, Geneva: United Nations

United Nations Office of Public Information (1959a) *United Nations Review*, 5:9, Geneva: United Nations

United Nations Office of Public Information (1959b) *United Nations Review*, 6:1, Geneva: United Nations

van den Dries L., Juffer F., van IJzendoorn M. H., Bakermans-Kranenburg M. J. and Lenneke R. A. (2012) 'Infants' responsiveness, attachment, and indriminate friendliness after international adoption from institutions or foster care in China: application of emotional availability scales to adoptive families', *Development and Psychopathology*, 24, pp 49–64

Verhulst F. C. and Verluis-den Bieman H. J. M. (1995) 'Developmental course of problem behaviours in adolescent adoptees', *Journal of American Academy of Child and Adolescent Psychiatry*, 34, pp 151–159

Vorria P., Papaligoura Z., Dunn J., van IJzendoorn M. H., Steele H., Kontopoulou A. and Sarafidou Y. (2003) 'Early experiences and attachment relationships of Greek infants raised in residential group care', *Journal of Child Psychology and Psychiatry*, 44:8, pp 1208–1220

Vorria P., Papaligoura Z., Sarafidou J., Kopakaki M., Dunn J., van IJzendoorn M. H. and Kontopoulou A. (2006) 'The development of adopted children after institutional care: a follow-up study', *Journal of Child Psychology and Psychiatry*, 47:12, pp 1246–1253

Weider H. (1978) 'On when and whether to disclose about adoption', *Journal of the American Psychoanalytic Association*, 26, pp 793–811

Xie H. L., Xie Z. K., Ye J., Yang X. J. and Qu J. (2010) 'Analysis of correlative factors and prevalence on China's youth myopia', *Zhanghua Yi Xue Za Zhi*, 90:7, pp 439–42

Younge G. (2010) *Who are we – and should it matter in the 21st Century?*, London: Penguin Viking

Appendix 1

Table of standard measures and their content

Questionnaire scale	Content	Comparison group/s
The General Health Questionnaire (GHQ12) (Goldberg *et al*, 1996)	Covers recent medical complaints and general health especially anxiety, depression and confidence	NCDS age-matched adopted and non-adopted UK-born women
The Malaise Scale (Rutter *et al*, 1970)	A commonly used self-completion scale for assessing psychological distress	NCDS matched adopted and non-adopted UK-born women
Life Satisfaction and Control	Three statements about life satisfaction, choice and control, plus a 10-point index asking how satisfied or dissatisfied the participant is with how life has turned out so far	NCDS matched adopted and non-adopted UK-born women
Mental Health Help-Seeking Index	Questions about psychiatric symptoms severe enough for the person ever to have consulted a specialist	NCDS matched adopted and non-adopted UK-born women
Rosenberg Self-esteem questionnaire (Rosenberg, 1965)	A self-report measure of global self-esteem, used to rate positive and negative attitudes and orientation towards the self	General population norms

Questionnaire scale	Content	Comparison group/s
Vulnerable Attachment Style Questionnaire (VASQ) (Bifulco et al, 2005)	Self-report measure used to detect view of adult social relationships by asking how participants feel about them-selves in relationship to others, for example social anxiety, confiding, trust and closeness	Community sample of low risk women
Parental Bonding Instrument (Parker et al, 1979)	Parenting styles (of adoptive mothers and fathers) as perceived by the participants looking back on their childhood and adolescence	Population norms
Modified Global Assessment of Functioning (GAF) Scale (Endicott et al, 1976)	Current overall level of functioning assessed by inter-viewer at end of research interview (3 categories)	Population norms
Community connectedness and self-regard questionnaires	Two new questionnaires were devised for this study to investigate identifications with Chinese communities and cultural practice and wider UK society. A third questionnaire measures self-regard in relation to Chinese appearance and whether this had changed over time.	None

Index